GW00771317

THE

Steps to Take for COMPLETE FORGIVENESS:

A Self Help Workbook

by

Dr. Jim Dincalci

The author of *How to Forgive When You Can't:*
The Breakthrough Guide to Free Your Heart & Mind
which is published in 9 languages, received 4 national awards, and
sold 100,000 copies worldwide.

Nobel Peace Prize Winner Bishop Desmond Tutu, and his
daughter, Mpho Tutu, acknowledged Dr. Jim for his contribution
to their book, *The Book of Forgiving.*

Copyright ©2021 by James Dincalci.

All rights reserved under the International and Pan-American Copyright Convention.

The material in this book may not be copied or reproduced in any form, in whole or in part, without the express permission of the author or The Forgiveness Foundation. Send requests for permission to use the material in this book to the Permissions Department, The Forgiveness Foundation International, fax to 262-244-3823 or RuahPress@forgivenessfoundation.org.

Profits from this book go toward –**Peace and kindness through forgiveness.**

Limit of Liability/Disclaimer of Warranty: While the publisher and author have used their best efforts in preparing this book, they make no warranties with respect to the completeness of its contents. Some of the advice and strategies contained herein may not be suitable for your situation. The information and opinions provided in this book are believed to be accurate and sound, based on the best judgment of the author, but readers who fail to consult with appropriate mental health professionals assume the risk of any problems. Neither the publisher nor author shall be liable for any loss of health or profit or any commercial damages, including but not limited to special, incidental, consequential, or other damages.

The Forgiveness Foundation books and products are available through our website. ForgivenessFoundationInternational.org

We also publish in a variety of electronic formats.

To contact us directly: USA - 919-929-0788; fax 262-244-3823.

ISBN: 978-0-9824307-6-7

<u>DEDICATION</u>

To the therapist, clergy, and counselors around the world who teach
how to forgive.
May their work continue through the ages
transforming our world to one of kindness.

To my daughter, Erica, and the young people of the world,
May this book bring you the means to a better future.

To all those who take care of people,
May this book lighten your heart.

To those who have been to hell from terrible trauma,
May this book help bring you peace.

To the forgiveness researchers around the world,
Without them this book would not be.

Please Note:
There are small letters and numbers at the end of some
sentences. These give the references to publications where the
information was found. See the "Endnotes" section at the end of
the book for the references in each chapter.

Readers should be aware that Internet Websites offered as
citations and/or sources for further information may have changed
or disappeared since the publication of this book.

TABLE OF CONTENTS

ACKNOWLEDGMENTS

To all my students and clients, I am grateful and hope that you, the reader, learn from their stories how they found what worked for them.

I am grateful to the forgiveness researchers around the world who are making forgiveness more accepted in psychology and the scientific community, and to the clinical researchers in Psychology, Sociology, and Neuroscience. Without their dedication to understanding human nature, we would not have the many tools available to help people lead happier lives.

My thanks and appreciation always to my friend and mentor, the late Dr. Angeles Arrien, Cultural Anthropologist, without whom I would not have had the forgiveness transformation I had that radically changed my life.

A very special thanks to Erica Dincalci, my daughter, for her daily support and being a valuable sounding board during the coronavirus pandemic, AND the beautiful work she did on the front and back covers, the inner formatting, and the hours we went over it.

I am grateful to the late Dr. Michael Berkes, friend, mentor, Psychology professor, MBA, for his foreword.

My profound thanks to Dana Eberhard, for her thorough work on editing this book. She made it much better with her wise suggestions on what to do. Though perhaps to my chagrin, I didn't follow everything she recommended.

A special thanks to Esther Luttrell for her editing and proofreading the middle phases of this workbook and her generous support in reworking it. Without her advice, the quality of this workbook would not nearly be as good as it is.

The workbook originally came about from a group of friends in Chapel Hill, NC, when I lived there. They were interested in a course in helping people forgive. My thanks to them for their desire for and initial work on this workbook, especially Dr. Eric Donaldson for his support without whom this workbook would not have been initiated, and for his for editing, building the model for working on upsets, proofing the book, and giving advice on placement of items in the chapters. And to Shawna Donaldson for her help on the above.

Thank you to Hana Whitfield, whose help was invaluable on the workbook's initial formatting, suggestions, and questions; and to Loralee Denny for proofreading the original draft of this workbook.

I am blessed to have first-rate friends around the world, including my centering prayer group in Tallahassee. All have been enthusiastic, supportive, and encouraging about this book, my teachings on how to forgive, and sending prayers thru my health challenge during the Covid-19 pandemic.

I am grateful to the legal professionals who are calling for the use of forgiveness and mercy to resolve hurtful situations and to the therapists, spiritual advisors, and church, mosque, and temple leaders all over the world who encourage its use every day.

A special thanks to Liz Gablehouse for her support through the years and for being the President of the Board of Director of The Forgiveness Foundation International.

With Love and Blessings to all the above,

Jim Dincalci

Tallahassee, Florida

ABOUT THE AUTHOR

For the past twenty-seven years, since his forgiveness transformation in 1993, Dr. Jim Dincalci has worked on methods to help people forgive, feel better, and heal their lives. His sources are from research in Neuroscience, Forgiveness Therapy, Stress Management, Conflict Resolution, Modern Psychology, Positive Psychology, Sociology, and Anthropology.

His education includes Doctorates in Cross-Cultural Religious Studies and in Divinity, Masters in Transpersonal Counseling Psychology, Graduate study in Clinical Health Care & Nursing, and Bachelor of Science in Pre-Medical Studies – Biology & Chemistry.

Besides his thirty-five years of private practice, his counseling experience includes working for the Hawaii Department of Health and the Department of Education as a clinical therapist in the state's school system. His experience also consists of three years of facilitating Domestic Violence and Anger Control groups for men and teens, three years of working in Drug and Alcohol rehab, two years as a Volunteer Law Enforcement Chaplain. For three years, he worked against Human Trafficking in Northern Florida as part of an executive committee of a coalition of agencies and organizations helping victims and educating the public and professionals on this crisis.

In 1974, Dr. Dincalci started presenting public seminars. Since then, he has done so at professional international, national, and state agency conferences, including the Campaign for Forgiveness Research in 2003 and two Rotary World Peace Conferences in 2017 and 2020. He has taught his forgiveness work in venues including counseling agencies, hospitals, schools, churches, plus, college and universities on the west and east coast, including Duke University, the Graduate Psychology Department at JFK University, Florida A&M University, and Florida State University. From 2001- 2005, he was an Assistant Professor in the Conflict Resolution Program at Sonoma State University, Cotati, CA.

He's trained in Trauma-Informed Care, and presented popular classes quarterly on stress management & meditation for 8 years at a community college in Santa Rosa., CA. His last work until Covid-19 was teaching: Resolving Resentment, Conflicts, and Stress at the Leon County jail and at a re-entry program for ex-offenders. He still does personal counseling for some who are presently in prison.

He is the founder and director of the Forgiveness Foundation International, a 501(c)3 since 2003 whose vision is building caring families & communities by healing blame, resentment & grudges.

His book, *How to Forgive When You Can't: The Breakthrough Guide to Free Your Heart and Mind,* is published in nine languages, has received four national awards and sold 100,000 copies worldwide. In it, he integrated his years of studying world religions, effective thought and emotional processes of psychology, Forgiveness therapy and sociology research, neuroscience, and inspirational viewpoints that all aid in forgiving.

FOREWORD

What Is There To Forgive?

Most of us get criticized, almost from birth, about our looks, our intelligence, our eagerness to learn, the knowledge we acquire, our worth, our lack of virtues. Our errors, our weaknesses, what we should not have done, what we did not do that we should have done, or did, but could have done better, far overshadow any good traits that may be noticed by our elders and so-called betters" during our childhood and adolescence. The list of such "observations for your own good" is endless and the damage they inflict remains painfully buried deep within.

Parents, teachers, and peers should be nurturing and encouraging us with their loving support, often do the opposite. Even more tragic are the misdeeds of so-called care-takers, who hurt the children both physically *and* emotionally instead of taking care of them, thus committing serious crimes that go mostly unpunished.

These are **toxic messages,** and we accept them, unchecked, in our innocence, because they come from the all-powerful grownups, and we are too young and inexperienced to defuse, let alone reject them outright. With repetition, and as we mature, these "truths" we accepted earlier are added to the ones we receive later. All are stored in our memory and remain deep in our subconscious, where they fester, mostly unknown to us, robbing us of our birthright to give and receive love while leading a happy and productive life.

With such a start, is it surprising that, as we learn to be social in various groups over time, we try to 'get even' with the world by being critical, judgmental, and hurtful ourselves? We put each other down; we ridicule, laugh, and diminish each other. Some believe that we do all this in "fun" and do not see the harm done. The toxic load that most of us carry gets piled on instead of being thrown off. Our employers, 'elders and betters,' products of their own less than happy childhoods, add their bits of insults to the injuries we suffer over the years, making the load of guilt even greater. Sadly, the "horse whisperers" are far outnumbered by the "horse whippers." (If you have not seen the movie, go see it!)

All this is done, for your own good!

Is it any wonder that we exhaust ourselves by worrying too much, working too hard, having too few rests and recreations and suffer from an endless list of ailments for which we are sold 'cures' from an ever longer list of drugstore "fixes"? Is it any wonder that we are as hard, if not harder on ourselves as our worst enemies are?

How many cups of coffee do you quaff a day just to stay awake? How many headaches do you ease with two, three and even more pills, when your doctors tell you that you have no physical causes for your aches?

When was the last time you had a truly restful night's sleep? Do you even know what your minimum need of sleep is? Did you know that it varies from 4 to 10 or more hours, for an *average* of 7, or 8? Did you know that lost sleep is not 'recoverable' by catnaps, but only by several fully restful nights?

Did you know that an estimated 40%-60% of Americans suffer from undiagnosed 'moderate to severe' depression? Why would we, one of the world's best fed, best housed, best protected, freest nations have cause to be depressed? How is it that we are rapidly becoming one the world's most overweight cultures?

When was the last time that you had a couple of weeks' worth of truly relaxed vacation during which you forgot about work and unfinished tasks and enjoyed life to the fullest? How about a couple of weekends every month?

Are there any people in your life, either past or present, about whom you choose no to think because it is too painful? Are there any disturbing thoughts which keep occurring, that you cannot figure out, or stop? Are those memories, for wrongs you have done, not just those done to you, disturbing to you, in your dreams, or when fully awake? Are there any occasions when, for no good reason, you seem to lose your 'cool' and flail out at someone you care for, hurting them against your will? Most, if not all of such outbursts are caused by un-resolved hurts and conflicts from the past. They can be resolved, if there is a will to do it, by forgiving yourself and others, through the method described in this book.

Don't you think it is high time for you to unload all that ballast of guilt and bad feelings, and start feeling free and joyous? It can be done! You can do it! All it takes is one step: start to read and follow this book's suggestions and exercises!

Michael Berkes, Ph.D. Psychology, MBA

The Beginning
An Initial Note from The Author on Using This Workbook

Hi! Welcome to *The Steps to Take for Complete Forgiveness*.

Through the years, I found that writing down key points that were significant to me from a book, helped me retain what was said. I've also found getting the upsets out of my head and onto paper helps calm me because it is the beginning of a commitment to deal with the upsets.

Writing down upsets from the past as you think of them and successful actions taken during this work is crucial to eliminating resentment, disappointments, and hurts.

If you want to use the workbook to keep notes, the publisher has provided some extra space after each question, and space in the workbook's margins, plus pages after each chapter and at the end of the book.

I like to sit at my computer or laptop and answer questions. Sometimes just a word or two as a reminder is sufficient. Other times, I write a lot. It is up to you.

In addition to the spaces in the workbook, I hope you buy a journal, something nice you will enjoy using to keep notes on your progress, and any ideas you get along the way. Date your entries so you can see the progress that you have made. Some people say they enjoy doing the work more with a favorite pen.

It would also be excellent for answering the questions in the exercises in this workbook, if you find you need more space for writing.

It is important to start writing down a forgiveness list. You will need to do that while working on an upset to keep track of people and areas of negativity that come to your mind so that you can deal with them at the appropriate time. Often, beginning the forgiving process triggers memories of other people or situations where there are still resentments. A key reason for recordkeeping is to have a list of past upsets to ensure that you address them.

Situations will come up that you have not thought about for many years. The events may have been hidden as part of your mind's defenses to prevent mental anguish. However, if hurtful situation still upsets you in the present, it has not been healed. It will continue to affect you beneath the surface of your awareness until you take care of it.[1]

In her book, *Molecules of Emotion: The Science Behind Mind-Body Medicine*, researcher Dr. Candace Pert tells us that studies have shown that when trauma victims write about their experiences, physiological changes occur, such as increased blood flow and a boost for the immune system that can last for up to six months.[2] Thus, the victims are more likely to have positive emotional shifts.

All this work--the journal, the exercises, and writing--is to have you seek out things in your heart and mind that prevent your happiness. This is "mindfulness"—carefully observing the effect of your thoughts, feelings, and deeper states of perception to help you deal with stress and life itself.

Forgiving is simply letting go of an upset to relieve *you* of the self-inflicted torture of hate, resentment, guilt, and anger.

Chapter 1
Opening to A Different Way

In 1993, while driving to my home through a little redwood forested road in Northern California, I realized that my life was no longer worth living and that I wanted to end it.

I thought I had done everything right. I had a pleasant home in the country, a lovely and smart daughter, a master's degree in counseling psychology, and a supportive community of friends. I cared about helping people. I was spiritual, but I had failed to become a person I respected because I was so miserable. My spirituality—so essential to me for years and a source of security and peace—was gone.

Even though I had studied various religions, psychologies, and cross-cultural healing methods for the previous 30 years, was a psychotherapist and taught different classes on these subjects in graduate schools, I could not help myself. I didn't know what to do to find relief from my misery and hopelessness. Forgiveness was not part of my life. Even my professional training didn't include forgiveness training.

Later on, different teachers and teachings guided me and certainly helped, but my upset feelings from 17 years of Post-Traumatic Stress Disorder (PTSD) always returned. I lived with anger, hate, resentment, and depression for so long, I thought they were normal. Even at that moment, when my life hit rock bottom and I felt so empty inside, I didn't think forgiveness was the answer because I accepted the same old justifications not to forgive that most people agree with (The Myths of Forgiveness that we will address soon). Consequently, I couldn't let go of the trauma and abuse I had experienced earlier in my life, though I did try!!

With all my anger and self-centeredness, I hadn't been that nice with either of my wives. But of course, it was their fault, I concluded in my delusional thinking.

At that point of utter despair and hopelessness, while I was driving home on that old redwood-tree-bordered road, I considered that my anger was destroying me rather than being a source of positive energy. At home in my little cottage, I started searching my mind for something that would help. Though I felt the best solution was to kill myself, I had learned that suicide has terrible effects on the children left behind. I did not want to do that to my little girl.

So, I searched for answers to get out of my hopelessness. Needing a miracle, I read the preface to A Course in Miracles. While reading it, I realized that I must forgive every past and present upset to experience God as Unconditional Love. My inspiration to forgive came from that idea that struck my heart to experience again the sense of deep love and joy that I yearned for and felt many times in my younger years.

When I use the term "love," I'm not talking only about love for a husband, wife, romantic partner, friend, or family member, but something beyond even those. It is often called "agape love," the highest form of love, considered Divine and Heavenly, which necessarily transcends human love and yet extends to one's fellow humans.[1]

The key that set me free that day in 1993 was forgiving all upsets I could think of. In one day, my happiness and appreciation for life returned! The change was miraculous, for love seemed to radiate to and from me. Love and joy have remained with me through the years, except for certain times when I couldn't forgive. When I encountered an upsetting person, love and joy disappeared until I had done a thorough letting go of my upsets with that person. Those times taught me more ways to help myself and others forgive.

Since I am far from being a saint, maintaining this joy and peace experience takes daily inner work, sometimes hourly, because I still get upset and angry about how terribly people treat each other. However, because the experience of joy and love are more important to me than anger and being upset, I let go of upsets to regain those positive experiences and work toward how I can improve my perspective.

My years of studying to become a psychotherapist, learning cross-cultural healing methods from wise teachers, counseling others, doing my inner work, and meditating, have enabled me to let go of my upsets pretty quickly, finally. I've written this workbook to help you master the techniques for letting go of resentments and grudges for yourself and others to make life better for you.

Self- Sabotage

I don't know why it is that many of us have something inside us that sabotages us. We know from brain research that the brain lies to us for our protection. Protecting us is its job. It's a self-support mechanism that helps us survive.[2] In fact, in dangerous situations, survival instincts will overcome our critical thinking, and we will probably react by fighting, fleeing, or freezing in some way.

I've certainly had these "take-overs" since I was a kid. Eventually, the "real" me would come back, and relaxing and thinking more clearly, I would again feel OK about life.

As part of our human experience, our minds find many ways to protect us, especially by convincing us to blame other people. I get it! Blaming others makes us right and others wrong, which protects us even when we're wrong. But why does that protection "go wrong" to the point that some people commit suicide or live lives of quiet desperation or worse? That's not self-protection at all; rather, it is sabotage. Why is that? What is that?

I haven't been able to answer those questions fully in my 75 years. But in 1993, driving home alongside the redwood trees on a country road, that sabotaging part of my mind finally won. The only way out, I determined, was to kill myself. The depression, anger, and self-blaming side of myself triumphed.

Through the ages, all sorts of reasons have been proposed for why we have a sabotaging side that can destroy us and others. The explanations range from evil spirits or the Devil to multiple personalities and psychopathological disorders. Modern psychology prefers not to separate those actions from us, instead, they call it part of our "ego." Further, brain science experts talk about reactive parts of the brain below the surface of our awareness that separate from our conscious awareness.[3] Some of these explanations help some people and not others. But there are solutions and safeguards—mindfulness, forgiveness, facing our fears, and gratitude, to name a few, which quiet those sabotaging parts of us and prevent them from dominating us. Whether you might call those hijackers or hackers that take our joy away doesn't matter. What does matter is taking action about whatever it is that can sabotage the healthy, happy part of us.

This book is the result of the quest for survival, joy, and love. It's the result of the pioneers who have studied our experiences and published them in professional research articles and books around the world to give us answers leading to being more content in our lives.

What Forgiving Really Is

What is forgiveness, and how can we reach that state of mind and heart when we are traumatically upset with another person, group, or even ourselves?

Forgiveness means "to stop blaming or being angry with someone for something they have done, or to ask someone not to be angry with you."- The Cambridge International Dictionary of English.

Forgiveness is:

- For you, not for the perpetrator. It allows *you* to live in freedom and joy, regardless of what has gone before.

- A process for letting go of the negative emotions and thoughts that produce depression, resentment, and anger so that peace of mind can lay a foundation for happiness.

- A skill developed through stages leading to increasing levels of awareness.

- The key to achieving your goals and making them a permanent part of your life.

A prominent forgiveness researcher, Dr. Robert Enright, and The Human Development Study Group noted a chief factor in defining forgiveness: positive feelings, opinions, and behavior toward the one being forgiven.[4]

In the twenty-seven years since I began doing this work, I've found that simply thinking of the person positively, sending them frequent prayers and love, and looking at how I might be grateful to them, makes a tremendous difference in releasing hostile feelings.

Here is an exercise I do daily that you can try. I rest in the love I have for people. I just sit in it, resting in it, feeling it in my heart. If you can do that: send it to your mother or father, grandmother or grandfather, or your brothers and sisters, your children, or good friends, even loved ones who have died.

A Simple Way to Understand Forgiveness

In forgiving a financial debt, the debtor no longer owes you the money. It is the same in forgiving a person or situation – they no longer owe you what you want or expect from them. Your expectation could be as intense as wanting to watch them die a painful death or as simple as receiving an apology. Often, it is wanting them to feel the pain you have felt. Forgiving means you let go of what you think or feel another owes you for what he, she, or they did to you.

One truth that has survived through centuries and has been applied worldwide is: *"Forgive us our debts, as we forgive our debtors."* If you can say that portion of the Lord's Prayer and truly mean it, truly mean that you have forgiven your debtors, then you are well on your way to conquering anger and resentment.

Here is an exercise for you.

Think about one person you are upset with.:

1. What punishment do you feel they deserve? Their debt to you is what you expect from them but haven't yet received. Do you simply need an apology from them? Or public humiliation the way they humiliated or angered you or destroyed your reputation? Or should they all grovel on their stomachs to you in grief? Or hang by their toes for three days? Or get beaten? Or watch their execution?

2. Write down what you think the person owes you. No one is going to read this but you, so let it all out. You can be as vicious as you like.
    Note: If you are working on forgiving *yourself*, you are looking for what you owe the other person or what you owe yourself or those close to you.

3. After you've finished writing down everything you want to say, think about if this is what you want from him or her. Is this the justice you wish for and from them?

4. Imagine how you will feel after your punishment. Will it truly make you happy to see the other person blamed and shamed? Will it completely solve your issue with the person? Will it bring you more success in life? Be honest.

5. How likely is it that you will see the desired punishment administered and the behavior change?

6. How long are you willing to wait for it to happen?

7. Will hauling around a heart full of bitterness get you what you want?

8. Are you willing to let this upset go? If not, what is it that you want?

9. Review what you learned from doing this exercise, as it might give you greater insight into your situation and maybe even reveal patterns around your thinking. These patterns are significant. When you find one, it gives you a more in-depth understanding of why you might be holding onto an upset, either with yourself or others.

Letting go of the debt does not mean you should not take care of yourself. Always take care of yourself. Stay Safe! You might ask yourself: By forgiving your offender, how can you take care of yourself so that this doesn't happen again?

Mercy

The most popular definition for mercy used throughout google is "compassion or forgiveness shown toward someone whom it is within one's power to punish or harm." In fact, it is so common that I cannot find the original source. Mercy is an important word to help describe forgiveness. This definition is essential in our understanding of forgiveness. Mercy, like forgiveness, is undeserved.

Sometimes, forgiveness and mercy are split up. For example, forgiveness involves overcoming anger and resentment; and mercy is withholding harsh treatment that one has a right to inflict.[5] I combine the two because forgiveness is giving up the harsh treatment you have the right to inflict. This is akin to "forgive us our debts as we forgive our debtors."

The Types of Forgiveness

For some, it is easier not to look at all the negative influences in a situation and just decide to forgive. That decision, a difficult one, I call direct forgiveness. It is often influenced by accepting a belief in Divine Love and Forgiveness, or the non-blaming condition of Nature. But, many of us cannot make that direct decision to forgive; it doesn't even seem possible.

If a person experiences great emotion around an upset, forgiving is often too difficult. Merely deciding to forgive can open you to *false forgiveness*--where you intend to forgive yet still resent and maybe even seek retribution in some way. Initially, if you decide to forgive without going through some sort of inner work, often the forgiveness decision must be repeated frequently to address the emotional turmoil that has not been released.

Today, most research, therapy, and spiritual counseling tries to move the person to the point of deciding to forgive.[6] This book and its exercises are for those who are not able to make that decision easily. It addresses how to permanently resolve resentment and guilt. As you read and do the exercises, you will find that your upset will change, and forgiveness sometimes will simply happen.

My Goal for This Book

To set forth a plan of action that enables the reader to forgive herself or himself and others effectively is the goal of this book. I aim to provide the reader with a forgiveness toolkit of techniques, perspectives, and exercises from tried-and-true, time-honored practices used for decades in Psychology, Sociology, Stress Management, Conflict Management, and Reconciliation developed at some of the world's finest research institutes.

What I have found significant in the past 25 years is the advent of Positive Psychology. It emphasizes the importance of faith, optimism, hope, resilience, emotional intelligence, spirituality, forgiveness, self-affirmation, happiness, quality of life, and social support, instead of the traditional focus on deficiencies and pathology.[7]

I am giving you this toolkit of methods. As with any toolkit, you use what you need at the time. It is the same with forgiving. You won't be using all the methods or questions. Gaining skills with the appropriate ones gives you information about when to use them and how to use them for different situations. Sometimes I need to step into the other person's shoes to get their perspective on why they did what they did. At other times, I can see there is nothing to forgive because the person just did what they were programmed to do given their situation. Then, my primary tool is to shift my mind to one of peace as opposed to one of shame, blame, or regret.

I provide many exercises throughout the book from my own experience drawing from over fifty years of work in professional therapies teaching in universities, hospitals, public seminars, colleges, agencies, and international conferences. As an assistant professor at Sonoma State University between 2001 and 2005, I taught a "how to forgive" course. At that time, psychotherapists took my course and told their clients to take it. I even had friends call me to say their therapist gave them my class notes to help them forgive. That was a strong incentive for me to publish my first book, *How to Forgive When You Can't: The Breakthrough Guide to Free Your Heart and Mind.*

I have continued to learn what works and what doesn't. I read all the research articles and books that I can, not only on forgiveness and neuroscience but also on other clinical research in psychology, sociology, and even anthropology, to make it easier for you to help you do this work.

You can use this workbook for a single difficult situation. It can also address a lifetime of negative experiences and emotions. It gives a format to work from and the secrets and essentials I've found to help people forgive more easily. I include over forty different forgiveness techniques and exercises to enable you to remove past resentments, grudges, and guilt. Please read this workbook in sequence as each chapter builds on the previous one.

My Search for What Works

When I started teaching forgiveness twenty-seven years ago, I thought all I needed to do was give people tools, and they would do the rest. I was wrong! Even though people say they need to forgive, they don't do it. They often feel they have too much to forgive or that forgiving is too difficult to do alone. They believe, as I did at one time, the justifications, and emotional defenses against forgiving. These need to be dispelled first before most people are willing to forgive. I will help you do that for yourself in this book.

Research Results on the Power of Forgiving

Here are some facts about the results of forgiving.

Research conducted at prestigious universities shows that forgiveness results in increased cardiovascular functioning and lower blood pressure and heart rate.[8] Research also shows:

- an increase in psychological and emotional well-being,
- less anxiety, anger, and stress,
- reduction in depression and hopelessness,
- more confidence and higher self-esteem
- increased energy and uplifted spirits.

These qualities were observed in extensive and separate research projects. In many instances, even more positive qualities became apparent.[9]

Journal Exercise

1. How does the *thought* of forgiving make you feel? The question is not about any one person in particular; it is about the idea of forgiveness itself.

2. Include the emotions and feelings that come up, whether positive, negative, or neutral.

3. What is it about the thought or idea of forgiveness that makes you feel this way?

Forgiveness Therapy is beneficial for treating these:
- Anxiety disorders, Panic disorder, Obsessive-compulsive disorder, Bipolar Disorder, Social phobia
- Substance-abuse and eating disorders; Impulse-control disorders such as gambling, pyromania, and kleptomania
- Personality disorders, such as paranoia, borderline, histrionic and narcissistic
- Any condition where strong anger is involved.[10]

➢ Do any of these situations have anything to do with you, your family members, or friends?

Journal Exercises on Forgiveness Results

To help you look more deeply at your inspiration and desires, please write out your answers to each of these key areas of healing by forgiving. These are from research articles quoted in Dr. Fredric Luskin's book, *Forgive for Good: A Proven Prescription for Health and Happiness.*[11]

Happier relationships

1. What could you do or say that would improve an existing relationship, whether it is with a spouse, parent, siblings, or someone else?

2. How would you go about doing that? What forgiving could you do?

Positive Results with Children

- How could you teach your child, children, or grandchildren to forgive more often?

Improved Spiritual Well-Being

- What, if anything, is there to forgive in your past that has to do with religion, God, or a Higher Power.

Dealing with Marriage and New Relationships   Statistics show that second and third marriages are not likely to be more successful than the first one. Therefore, identifying and forgiving the hurtful deeds done to you or by you in your past intimate relationships is imperative. Also, looking at your family relationships while you were growing up is essential.

1. Write down any hurtful or angry memories that came up as you read the above passage.

2. Add the people involved in that situation to your existing list if they are not already on it.

Physical Healing

Hostile, angry relationships hurt one's health. Many have reported how their health improved after forgiving those who caused them to hate or be angry or bitter.

If you are sick or have recent or chronic pain, be brutally honest with yourself as you write answers to these questions in your journal:

1. When did your physical problem start?

2. What was going on in your life at that time?

3. Who or what (such as an organization or event) might you need to forgive in that situation?

Self-Forgiveness

All the exercises and suggestions in this workbook can be applied to self-forgiving also. Gaining self-forgiveness is vital to your emotional happiness, spiritual connection, and physical health.[12] Research in self-forgiveness shows that you will experience increased positive self-esteem, well-being, mental health, greater agreeableness, and decreased depression and anxiety.[13]

Through the years, I've heard people say that you need to forgive yourself before you can forgive others. That is not always true. I have found for myself and many others I've worked with that it is frequently easier to forgive others than ourselves. Even so, researchers also found that a person's mental health was more strongly related to self-forgiveness than forgiveness of others.[14] So, exercise your forgiveness muscle on others, and it will start to work on your self-perspective too.

Sometimes a person can't forgive themself because of the harm they did to another or others. Then forgiveness needs to be earned or received from another. Later in the book, I include ways to do that, even if the person hurt is no longer alive.

If you are working with self-forgiveness, reword the questions I give throughout the book to fit your situation.

Notes

Chapter 2
What Prevents and Inspires Forgiveness

As we look around the world, un-forgiveness is out of control. Wars worldwide pit countries against countries, one religion against another, even people of the same faith and ethnic group killing each other. Though there is plenty of research and methods to deal with opposition and conflict management, we often don't use that information, choosing instead to harm and even destroy those who disagree with us.

Clinical research in forgiveness and the brain has given us concrete evidence, perspectives, and methods of the most effective ways to deal with resentment, guilt, grudges, and anger. The problem is that people must be willing to do the work of forgiving. Most are not. This workbook attempts to make a difference for those who feel there must be a better way.

By following this book's flow and applying your awareness to the questions, stories, and concepts, you build your ability to forgive. Inevitably, just by going through the book, your forgiving skills will increase more than you might think. Thus, you will be happier and have better relationships. You don't have to worry about doing all the questions. Just apply yourself to look at them and consider possible answers. Over the years, my experience leaves me no doubt that your skills in forgiving will significantly increase, and your life will change for the better, for some, radically.

A Personal Forgiveness Survey

1. Are there situations in your life where you often have feelings of guilt?

2. Have you done things you regret that are still upsetting you?

3. Are there people you want to make suffer as much as you have because of their actions?

4. Are there people you think of that you hate? Or resent?

If you have answered any of those questions with yes, then this workbook will make a big difference in your life. If these questions don't pertain to your situation, but you are reading this to help someone else forgive, great. You will gain many helpful methods that will empower you to help even the most upset person. (Many of my questions are *you* oriented. Just think of them as questions to ask the person you are helping.)

Probably the essential point to remember about forgiveness is that it is for your own benefit. It might help another when you forgive, but this book is concerned with you. You have the most to gain by forgiving others and yourself. You can always answer the exercises' questions so that they pertain to self-forgiving instead of the perpetrator, for sometimes you are your own offender.

When a person forgives, he or she brings peace into their part of the world. The more people who forgive and find its power, the more peace we can have in the world.

Forgiving is like exercising—the more you do it, the easier it becomes, and the better you are at it.

Though forgiveness is one of the highest functions built into the brain, the desire for justice is also built-in.[1] Therefore, we frequently feel that we at least need an apology from someone before we can forgive them, and often we expect much more. This expectation hinders forgiving because the "offender" might see the situation very differently. If you never get the apology, you will likely end up suffering from the stress hormones that the upset activates in your body.

Resentment initially gives us satisfaction like having chocolate, but researchers found that revenge does not really bring relief.[2]

Forgiveness Barriers and Progress

Here are a few areas that prevent forgiveness, which are seldom addressed when people try to forgive. All of these factors can cause us to remain miserable. I address all the blocks that keep us reluctant to forgive.

- The desire for justice and fairness is important to us, which plays against forgiveness. How do you deal with that real and fundamental desire for justice and fairness when you consider forgiving?

- There are over eight beliefs or myths that people hold that prevent forgiving that research identified years ago. These must first be addressed before a person is even willing to forgive. We will go over these in the next chapter. Pastors and religious teachers around the world hit up against these false beliefs. I hope this book can help them even more, to help others be more willing to forgive. I've had pastors give sermons and lessons from my earlier book.

- There are emotional defense mechanisms that can prevent forgiving.

- But a key one that I have observed these many years is the lack of willingness to face our fears. We will go into this much more later. Fear normally activates our fight-and-flight survival mechanisms and can easily shut off our critical thinking and positive emotional connections. Facing our demons is important to this work. I offer you many questions to help you look at what is going on inside instead of moving along with fear or anger running the show.

Neuroscience has given us deep insight into the brain's workings that have changed long-held assumptions about our thinking. These studies help us understand forgiveness. Thirty-five years of forgiveness research has given us untold data proving the power of forgiving on our mental and physical health and well-being that is only now coming into public awareness.

Forgiveness therapy research has helped us understand how to make forgiving more effective. Only since 2010, have I seen the typical psychiatrist or psychotherapist starting to become aware of the research on forgiveness therapy.

Take It Easy With This Work!

I encourage you to avoid jumping into dealing with the most difficult, abusive, or traumatic situation of your life right away. Take it easy. Deal with the easy stuff first. Learn more about the ins and outs of forgiving by reading and participating in the exercises suggested in this workbook. There is a comprehensive process mapped out for you to be successful in your desire to forgive.

You might find reading my book, *How to Forgive When You Can't,* helpful, but reading it is unnecessary unless you want to read real-life successes and examples of different techniques.

The Forgiveness Foundation International is developing programs and information to teach forgiveness methods to mental health professionals, and clergy, so check out our website, forgivenessfoundationinternational.org.

The workbook's perspectives will empower you to move past emotional blocks that prevent forgiving. Deep-seated resentments will likely take more work and may require using several different methods. If you run into difficulty, getting the help of a therapist can be invaluable.

Our combined experience in the Foundation has demonstrated that if you are willing to do this work and do the exercises, you will be free of your resentments, grudges, and guilt. We have experienced this level of forgiveness in our own lives and seen the transformation in others. This transformation is what we want for you!

In summary, this book provides the tools to help examine how to:

- resolve and get past the harmful ideas your mind holds onto.

- reduce stress and retrain your brain to be more positive.

- empower you to make positive and permanent changes in your life.

A variety of upsets, hurts, and resentments will also be addressed, accompanied by over forty forgiveness methods. If faithfully applied, these tools will bring about the ability to forgive completely. Exercises are provided to focus your time and energy on the critical task of doing the work.

Mindfulness

I define mindfulness as carefully observing the effects of your thoughts, feelings, and deeper states of perception to help deal with stress and life itself. It is integral to forgiving because it enables you to deeply look at all sides of an upset instead of attacking the other or justifying your actions. The questions I offer in each section of this book are specifically intended to examine what in your thoughts is preventing your happiness. You are giving yourself a fantastic tool, mindfulness, to look more deeply at what is causing upsets so that you can be content for the rest of your life.

Be Creative

Though I give questions, don't use them rigidly but as sparks in your mind. You might find another way to work with the question I give. Wonderful! For instance, I might say, "Describe what happened." But you might draw a picture, or if you like music, you might sing about it.

Making it fun can dissolve the upset a lot by viewing it in an amusing, creative, or unusual way. Laughter is always great medicine.

The Myths - Misunderstandings and Lies about Forgiveness that prevent a person from doing it -

Early on in teaching forgiveness, I discovered clinical articles that talked of misconceptions, which cause justifications against forgiving. These need to be dispelled before an adult or child is even willing to forgive.[3] For example, denying or minimizing what happened, condoning or excusing the offense, or trying to forget the wrong, are not true, but most people believe them.

The following are further descriptions.

Myth 1 – **I can't forgive because the person who caused the upset is deceased or no longer around.** Though they are gone, if the injury is still alive, it will continue to affect you. At some level, harboring any resentment, large or small, affects your life and interactions with people.

The purpose of forgiving is to relieve the self-inflicted injuries of hate, anger, and resentment. It is not dependent on the other person or their apology.

Questions to help you look deeper:
1. Are you still carrying the upsetting emotions even though the person is gone?

2. Are you still holding out for some justice that will never come?

3. Are you holding some hope for reconciliation that is unrealistic?

4. Is it time to let it go?

Myth 2 – I don't have to forgive because I never want to see them again! As with Myth 1, if we harbor resentment or hurt, the upset still lives. Forgiveness is not reconciliation, which is about building trust. They might not be trustworthy. If you don't want them in your life, that's fine. However, you can still forgive and even seek justice.[3a] You don't have to be a doormat.

Questions to help look deeper:
1. You might not want reconciliation, but is there something you do want from them? Perhaps for them to feel the pain you felt? Or maybe some justice?

2. Are you afraid of seeing them? If so, how can you set limits, not only on them but perhaps on yourself? Do you need to work on patterns in your life where you don't take care of yourself?

Myth 3 – If I forgive, I will be condoning or justifying their offense. You are not condoning or justifying by letting the upset go. You can forgive and set limits, as mentioned above. A drug abuser's family may forgive their behavior out of love and understanding but not condone drug misuse or unlawful behavior, such as stealing. The family can love and forgive the addict and still ask them to leave the house due to not condoning drug usage and the resulting **abusive** behavior or theft.

Questions to help look deeper:
1. How can you let go of the upset and still set limits on behavior?

2. Are there limits you need to set on your own behavior?

Myth 4 – They do not deserve it! You might be right; they might not. BUT, you forgive for yourself, for your benefit, and your peace of mind.

Questions to help look deeper:
1. Would you rather be right than happy?

2. Can you take care of yourself by setting boundaries, perhaps not even see the upsetting person, and still forgive?

Myth 5 - I just want to forget about it. Forgive and forget is a myth. The brain is not set up to forget. Real forgiveness allows the upset to fade in the mind because it is no longer activated. Trying to forget about a hurt is not forgiveness but denial. The negative results of denial influence you in a gradual, subtle way, but with harmful effects under the surface of your mind, causing trouble for you when you aren't even aware of it.[4]

Questions to help look deeper:

Go to the feelings list in the Appendix to help you identify other emotions you might not be aware of that are part of an upset.

1.   Think of your situation and read the list of negative feelings to see if any of them cause a shift. One often will.

2.   Read through the positive feeling list while thinking of an upset.

You might find that the upset will go away. You can do this anytime. Reading positive emotions shifts your mind out of its negativity.

Myth 6 – Before I forgive, I need an apology! You may wait forever for an apology because the person may have a different perspective. If you want reconciliation, then that is different and requires the deep work of rebuilding trust. Forgiveness is an excellent first step.

A question to help look deeper:
- What can you do personally to let the upset go without the apology?

Myth 7 - I cannot forgive because they keep doing it! Admittedly, this can be a more difficult situation to deal with. Still, I have seen people handle the situation with forgiving who gained some peace of mind, especially when they could not or chose not to leave a challenging relationship. Remember, take care of yourself.

Questions to help look deeper:
1. Do you know someone who keeps hurting you?

2. Is it because the person does not know better? Or is it because he/she delights in hurting you again and again?

3. What happens when you try to separate yourself from the hurt, not the person.

4. If the person does not know better, can you consider talking with the individual gently about it? What would be the safest way to do that? For example, in the presence of someone else besides the offender?

If you are experiencing a physically or emotionally abusive situation, you must protect yourself first. See the next myth also.

➤ Get away from the abuse. Get safe. Cities often have "safe houses" where a woman can go with her kids. Call a women's counseling center or the police for more info on these.

➤ Go to a health care practitioner, abuse counselor, etc., who can help you. Talk to them about your situation. The time to forgive is after you are safe and away from the abuse.

Myth 8 - **They will just hurt me again if I forgive and go back!** Why would you go back? Take care of yourself. Forgiveness is not "turning the other cheek!" Jesus' original meaning was strength in faith and remains a misunderstood and disagreed-upon concept because, at other times in the Bible, Jesus says to take care of yourself. Theologically, this passage has been argued about for centuries with no absolute interpretation.

When a relationship has physical or emotional abuse, it is in deep trouble. Outside help is needed. Limit-setting on the abuse is urgent. This is not work you should do alone. You must protect yourself. Physical and emotional abuse needs to be stopped.

Questions to help look deeper:
Look at the upset you are working on.
• Can you forgive and set limits so that you are not hurt again?

Myths of Forgiveness Detection to Help in Forgiving

Questions to help look deeper

Recall a situation in your life where you have been unsuccessful in forgiving another person.

1. Look and see if one of the Myths of Forgiveness stands in the way of your being able to forgive. Write down the myth and why you feel this way? Put down all the explanations and justifications you can find.

2. Would dispelling that myth allow you to see the situation from a different perspective?

3. Can you forgive the other person now?

The Struggle between Religion and Psychology

People in most religious realms have good intentions and some training in helping people forgive. Over the years, I have talked with many of them about the techniques that work for them. Looking at the prevalence of violence around the world, both between religious groups and even among them, it appears that there is a lot of room for improving religious teachings about forgiveness.

Why is this? There is speculation that in the mid-to-late 1800s, most psychologists rejected church control and its interpretation in mental health.[5] As a result, forgiveness was lost to the professional therapy community for decades. None of the noted psychologists up to the 1980s addressed forgiveness. It is only starting to be used more today.[6,7]

Finding a therapist or doctor who understands and teaches forgiveness is not easy. One of the reasons I first published my book in 2009, *How to Forgive When You Can't: The Breakthrough Guide to Free Your Heart and Mind*, was to assist professionals, clergy, pastoral counselors, and laypeople to do a better job of helping others learn how to forgive.

Research in forgiveness and the brain has given us excellent perspectives and methods to help us deal with conflict, resentment, guilt, grudges, and anger. The problem is that people must be willing to use these methods and perspectives. Since you've picked up this book, you are interested in making a difference for your life and those around you. This book will make a difference for those of you who feel there must be a better way to survive in the world, be happy, and deal with stress better.

Trauma and Abuse

Facing deep trauma and abuse can evoke enormous levels of shock, anger, grief, and fear. It is vital to be patient with yourself, take care of yourself, and take it easy, as I said earlier. Only address trauma when you have enough experience doing this work and enough time to work on each stage of forgiveness before moving onto the next.

A person dealing with trauma and abuse must first feel safe. That can take a while. We don't even recommend jumping into forgiving until you, or the person you are helping to forgive, feels safe and calmed down.

The long-term effects of stress and bullying and dealing with them effectively are covered later in the book. You may want to start with the heavy emotional and traumatic issues that you already carry. However, even though you feel a sense of urgency to jump in, take it easy. Your ability to face and deal with hurtful memories will keep rising the further you go doing the exercises in this book.

I recommend working on less volatile upsets first. In weightlifting, you don't just start with lifting 150 lbs. You work up to it gradually. As you tackle the easier hurts with forgiveness, you will gain skill, raise your ability to deal with resentments more efficiently, and find the strength and momentum to tackle the more difficult ones with success. Your ability to face and deal with hurtful memories will keep improving the further you go, and you'll find that you will be able to forgive even incidents you considered unforgivable, the "200-lb." ones.

Please note: If you find a situation too difficult or too painful to resolve on your own, work with a therapist trained in **"Trauma-informed Care."** Its practices are specifically used by therapists who work with people who have experienced Human Trafficking, Sexual Abuse, Adverse Childhood Experiences (ACEs), and Toxic Stress. They take into account the harm that has occurred. Trauma-informed care comprises victim-centered practices that allow the victim to begin working through the trauma.[7a] It is done only by highly trained therapists and is for adults and children.

Be Aware of The Small Shifts of Heart and Attitude

The last thing I want to address in this chapter is always to be aware of the small shifts of heart and attitude that you will experience as you or forgive.

I call them "felt-shifts." They will occur as you make progress through this book. They come as a slight feeling of relief, a change of attitude, a sudden thought or feeling, for example, that the wrongdoer is not such a bad person after all. It's a shift in perspective accompanied by a physical sensation of some sort, even a smile or an Aha!. These are the little shifts you want to watch for, as they can come unexpectedly.

This forgiveness work is not an intellectual process but integrates mind, emotions, and body. You work for that shift. That is how you know that you or they have forgiven in some way. Even if they decide to forgive, you know it's happened when there is a felt shift. Every item of the over 900 things I needed to forgive had a *felt-shift*. I didn't wonder if I forgave or not, I knew.

I felt those shifts as a lessening of tension in my body and my mind. I felt lighter. For that reason, I like to use the example of carrying around thick battle armor, such as the knights used in the Middle Ages. This *armor* metaphor is not far from the truth, energy-wise, in our minds. This protection that we carry gets heavier and heavier as we go through life trying to protect ourselves from pain and suffering caused by others or our own actions. With this *armor*, it's harder to enjoy life and people because it's there to protect us from life and people. Those protections work but at the cost of losing a deep connection to Love, Peace, and Joy that we all have available to us.

These shifts are significant because they generate positive energy, enabling enormous positive changes to take place in your mind and heart. Once you experience a felt-shift, you are probably finished with that person or at least that one upset.

◆ Have you already experienced some changes? Write them in your journal

◆ In the future, as soon as you feel a felt-shift, write about it in your journal

Having A Sense of Safety

When our brain is not under significant stress, threat, or pressure, it works best.[8] Therefore, make sure that you are in a safe, comfortable environment when you do this work. Only in a safe environment can the brain's fight and flight mechanism deactivate, allowing the relaxed but alert parasympathetic nervous system to come forward.[9] You want your emotions to be calm so that your higher thinking abilities can work in sync and harmony on unforgiven and stressful situations.

Without feeling safe, conflict resolution or reconciliation cannot occur with any degree of success. [10]

A woman or child in a domestically violent situation needs to feel safe, or else she and her child will be unhappy, for they will never know the next time her husband/partner will be violent. When workers do not know if their job is secure, it's a formula for discontent.

Journal Exercise:
a. Look at the type of environment that would be best to do this work - one that is safe and does not have distractions.

b. If your home or office does not fit, find another. It could be at a friend's house, a library, and even a quiet park bench.

Try Asking "What" Questions

Please note. Asking yourself "*why*" you have the thoughts, feelings, and situations that you do serves no purpose. Researcher and Organizational Psychologist Dr. Tasha Eurich tells us that w*hy* questions can focus us on our limitations, stir up negative emotions, and trap us in our past. Properly structured *"what"* questions help us see our potential, help us better understand and manage our feelings, and help us create a better future. Instead of asking *why* ask these questions: What's going on? What am I feeling? What is the dialogue inside my head? What is another way to see this situation?[11]

- What's going on?
- What are you feeling?
- What are you saying inside your head?
- What is another way to see this situation?

As you let go of the unforgiven upsets that affect your life, research shows you will have less stress at home and work, more energy, health, clear thinking, positive emotions and relationships, and a better spiritual outlook.[12]

Notes

Chapter 3
Important Preliminary Points

The Search for What Works

When I started teaching forgiveness, I thought all I needed to do was give people tools on forgiving, and they would take it from there. Even though people say they need and want to forgive, not only do the demands of their life get in the way, but I found there are also complex internal factors and social beliefs that prevent forgiving. Through the years, due to my passionate interest in what clinical research and neuroscience have taught us about how to forgive and be happy, we now have much better methods to help people forgive.

I call the results of my search *The Power Forgiveness Approach,* a complete system available to help people let go of anger, upsets, resentment, guilt, and fear from past and present hurts.

I call my approach "power" forgiveness for three reasons.

- ♦ It requires the power of your willingness and dedication to do this work successfully.
- ♦ It puts the power of your life back into your own hands (Never again do you have to live your life as a victim); and
- ♦ It is a set of methods for dealing with all your upsets so that your heart, mind, and soul are free to experience a Power greater than your—or my—small, fearful self.

As I outline it, the approach enables you to become completely free from past events that accumulate and contribute to your negativity. By releasing old hurts, you free your mind to focus on more positive and constructive ventures.[1]

In his novel on forgiveness, *By the River Piedra, I Sat Down and Wept,* Paolo Coelho tells us his personal experience with forgiving. "One morning, going from Death Valley in California to Tucson in Arizona, I made a mental list of everyone I thought I hated because they had hurt me. I went along pardoning them one by one; six hours later in Tucson, my soul felt so light and my life had changed much for the better."

His experience is much like what I did that day when my life hit bottom and was transformed through forgiving.

Success in Forgiving

Letting go of intense upsets does not come easily to most people, but we all can develop the skills necessary to forgive. It will take work and practice, so please do the exercises. We all come from exceedingly different perspectives. Therefore, different forgiveness solutions discussed in this workbook will be appropriate for different people.

Please take note: Often, we get excited by the possibility of making a life change only to get off to a good start and then stop a few days or a week later. I've seen this happen many times. People successfully forgive some upsets, and feel re-energized and happy, and take a break. The "forgiving momentum" can ebb, leaving other troubles to fester. Subtly, the state of negativity returns, and old habits re-establish the other upset neatly below the surface of our awareness where they will negatively affect us in the future. Burying old injuries is detrimental to your physical and mental health.

So, keep on forgiving. Don't let some pleasant feelings stop the process. Take a break, that's fine. But then come back to the forgiveness work because the transformation of your life is at the end of your list of upsets, not just after feeling good for a little time.

Use the energy you have regained from forgiving to work on the remaining upsets until they are all gone. Then you can live your life as a happy and free person. I promise.

Special Message: Forgiveness is not an easy path because it can open painful memories. Because of the confusion of the emotions connected to the subject, it is best to keep this work private. Don't tell others that you are working on forgiveness. Through long experience teaching this subject, it is also *imperative* not to tell someone you have forgiven him or her—unless they specifically asked for forgiveness in the past and you didn't give it. During this vulnerable time, you don't need to hear other people's unforgiven stories, risk others' criticism or ridicule, or upset others by telling them you forgave them when they might have thought you were the guilty party, which is not unusual!

The Real Consequence of Holding on to Upsets

People believe there is a benefit to not forgiving. Generally, people have a good reason for doing or not doing something. There is often a **payoff** for not letting go of the upset. Even though a decision we've made might not seem to be in our best interest, if we look deeply, we might find that we believed the choice was the best one possible at the time. Often, fight, flight, freeze, and hide brain reactions and stress influence us. Sometimes even, we don't notice how much an upset affects us.

Journal Exercise

Ask yourself:

1. How you benefit by keeping the upset going?

2. How does holding onto the upset help your life and make you *genuinely* happy?

3. Is being right more important than being happy and healthy?

4. What am I getting out of this upset? List the negatives and the positives.

5. What is happening to the people closest to me by my holding onto the upset?

6. In my life, how strong are love, peace, and joy?

7. Could forgiving this situation increase my happiness and that of those around me?

Clarification on Acceptance and Forgiveness

Several years ago, I discussed Acceptance and Forgiveness in a Los Angeles NPR radio interview.

Acceptance is a natural step in forgiving because you must look realistically at the situation and feelings going on around the upset, but that doesn't necessarily result in forgiveness. The best definitions for *accept* that I've found were

*   to stop denying or resisting (something true or necessary), i.e., "The truth is sometimes hard to *accept*."
*   to admit that you have or deserve (something, such as blame or responsibility), i.e., to *accept* blame or "I *accept* responsibility for the accident."[2]

You can accept what happened, and even accept blame and responsibility and not feel forgiven for an offense you did or not feel forgiving toward another. Acceptance carries us to the point of being willing to forgive. But forgiveness – letting the upset go – is the change that is needed. It relieves the body and mind of the upset, returning you to a natural connection to life.

I've seen people completely accept the negative state of their life and their depression. They wallow in it, "acceptingly" remaining unhappy, depressed, and unpleasant to be around. It's my experience that depression dissolves when real and complete forgiveness is done. Even my meditations went much deeper after my forgiveness transformation.

In learning, "priming" is where one subject is associated with another. For example, to teach about a banana, you would remind them about a similar subject like yellow first.[3] Acceptance is wonderful for priming forgiveness. In the 12 steps an NPR interview I mentioned, acceptance is often considered forgiveness because it has been primed for forgiving so well.

Journal Exercise:
1. Journal all the things you accept but are unhappy about, sad about, or regret happened in your life.

2. What can you accept about each person who did those?

3. What can you not accept?

4. What might you forgive concerning any of those people?

These questions will give you more items you can work on when you learn more forgiveness methods as you go along in the book.

Our Areas of Focus

Certainly, our lives are affected by the complex inter-working of these six areas: a) thoughts, b) feelings, c) body, d) environment and surroundings, e) social and relational connection to others, and f) spiritual focus. They are all important. We depend on each working together for our happiness. For example, food affects not only our bodies but our moods. Too much of one food can also affect our social interactions; vitamins we take for the body can also affect our mood and our desire to interact socially. Meditation for physical relaxation can lower anxiety and even blood pressure. Forgiveness alone also can radically change these six areas of focus for the better.

Limits and Boundaries

You can ask a person who upset you to change, or you can rid them from your life. But if you don't clean up what is unforgiven, that upset will keep showing up, causing stress.[4] You can decide if you want the person in your life but remember forgiveness does not depend on them, only on you.

Forgiveness requires letting go of upsets that harm you and then setting healthy boundaries and limits for yourself and others, limits that keep you safe and happy.

True forgiveness frees your heart, soul, and mind. However, research suggests that forgiveness requires trust that the other person will not hurt you again and that you feel safe.[5] Therefore, forgiveness is not only letting go of the hurts and upsets; it's also about setting responsible boundaries with those that hurt you so that you are not hurt again. Sometimes, those boundaries are difficult to establish. The purpose of this work is to empower you to live your life without ever being a victim again.

Advances in neuroscience that focused on revenge and reward have revealed some significant facts that may explain our natural inclinations to seek revenge, hang onto negativity, and avoid forgiveness.[6]

Dealing with Big Events and Situations

Sometimes our resentments involve many things done over a long period by a perpetrator. You deal with that person the same way you would deal with an organization, church, or country.

Your first action is to break down the whole situation or event into its parts—each person involved, what each person did or said, etc. This "breaking down" procedure is essential; otherwise, the situation might be too much to manage. You don't eat a steak whole—you cut it up into bite-size pieces. It's the same with a big unforgiven situation, people, or events.

If it's one person who harmed many times, write down all the different times you can think of that the offender wronged you. You might think that this will be difficult. But you'll find that **facing the exact factors of the upset will be freeing**, for it will no longer be in your subconscious where it negatively affects you in ways you don't even realize. If it is too intense, work on one situation at a time, or find a therapist, psychologist, or pastoral counselor to help.

Concerning a large organization like a church, country, etc., write down each person in that organization that caused you hurt. Work toward identifying WHO—the person or people that represent the injustice in your thoughts. Usually, upsets will stem from the actions of only one person or just a few, not the whole organization or even country.

Your Search for What Works

As you travel this forgiveness road, you may find that you need additional information to understand and resolve a specific hurt or trauma you experienced. If so, search the library, explore the Internet, see a therapist, and talk to friends.

You may also find that, while some of these forgiveness tools work very well for you, others don't. *Use those that work.* Write them down in your journal as you go and build your toolkit of useful forgiveness techniques. By doing this, when you get upset, you can refer back to your journal to help you.

So, why is forgiveness so complicated that it takes a process, a whole lot of willingness, and a ton of action? We address the roadblocks to forgiving by asking and addressing these questions:

- Why do we hold onto resentments and hatred that ruin our lives and the lives of others?

- What are the thought patterns and emotions that keep us from forgiving?

- Why do we listen to our own negativity, even when we sense that it is not good for us?

By answering these questions, you will address the main obstacles to forgiving, which will provide the willingness you need to engage in the Power Forgiveness approach fully!

HELPFUL METHODS

Create or Generate Positive Feelings Toward the Other

Since positive feelings toward the person being forgiven are important for forgiveness, I've found we can short-cut the work of forgiving by starting with positive feelings for ourselves or another.

The exercise below is the most effective tool I've found in my fifty years of counseling. I'm astounded at its power to help people feel better in a short time. For that reason, it is used all over the world, with variations of it in several religions. It predates Christianity and Buddhism. The Indian saint, Mahatma Gandhi, was a strong advocate of its use. It is also known as Maitrī or Metta.[7] A good book on the subject is *Loving-kindness: The Revolutionary Art of Happiness* by Sharon Salzberg. The term "lovingkindness" occurs 248 times in the Hebrew Bible.[8]

In recent years, people in my counseling, classes, and groups have had significant success in feeling better about people and life by using the following affirmation or blessing. I put together these blessings from the different Maitrī and Metta ones I found on the web.

This method directly addresses the well-being of another—the result of forgiving. Those who practiced it daily experienced significant positive changes in the brain and body, including lowered stress response and even reduced inflammation. Participants reported being more satisfied with their lives, having an overall sense of well-being, and experiencing fewer depression symptoms.[9] Research in 2016 showed positive emotions, positive social connections, and physical health influence as a result of this meditation.[10]

I've seen it help people heal when they hit tough times, even in drug and alcohol recovery and loss of a loved one. I've found, if you say it sincerely for others, and you can get the same blessing as someone saying it for you.

It is best to do it with your full intention and to visualize the result for the offender. The more you see the positive results for the person in your mind, the more helpful the affirmation can be for you.

In one of the most challenging forgiveness works I did in my life, I finally started making headway by using this affirmation for the person involved, saying it over and over for days. It worked. At first, I had to fake it, but I finally made it to where I wanted those things for the person. I realized that if that person really had what the affirmation or blessing intends, the situation would not have happened.

Do this. Initially, you don't have to say it for someone you are upset with but for someone you care about. It has the power to take your mind off being upset and stressed. Say it several times for someone you love and have affection for—mother or father or both, or a good friend—anyone you have good feelings for or want to have good feelings for.

May you be safe.
May you be well.
May you be happy.
May you be free from suffering.
May you be filled with love and kindness.
May you be filled with joy.
May you be at peace and at ease.

Adapt this affirmation in any way that you see fit. I have often shortened it to: "May you be safe, well, and happy. Free from suffering; Filled with loving-kindness, peace, and joy."

Also, for those who like to do positive affirmations – picturing the person in a positive state, you can say, "**You are** safe, well, and happy, Free from suffering..." etc.

Any variations are an excellent evening practice with anyone you are even a little bothered with during the day. If you can't think of someone, it is terrific to do for a person you love and appreciate to put yourself in a better mood.

Traditionally, it is done first for people we feel close to, then for those we are neutral toward, and then those we are upset with.

1. Write out the above blessing and can carry it with you. Better yet, consider what it would be like if your offender had those positive things happen.

2. When someone upsets your peace of mind, think of a loved one and say this blessing for them several times until you feel a shift in your heart about the situation.

I encourage eventually trying to say it for the person you are upset with. But that is difficult for many, so after you do it for a loved one several times, try doing it for someone you might see on the street or someone else who might come to mind. Perhaps make it a game by saying it for the offender's foot, then hand, etc.

If it is too hard to do for the offender, don't worry. You can benefit just by saying it for a loved one. Or you can say it for yourself by inserting

"May I" into all those statements. The point is for you and them to feel better and not stressed. Forgiving is easier with less stress.
A deeper investigation of the Lovingkindness work takes place in Chapter 10.

How Do You Know Forgiveness Was a Success?

After forgiving, you will still remember the event, but the negative emotions associated with it will be released or significantly weakened. Forgive and forget is a falsehood. The brain does not allow that.

To test if your forgiveness was a success, you can ask:

- "Can you think about the person easily, calmly, and without getting upset?"

- Is there anyone you say you have forgiven, but you haven't really?

Forgiveness wipes away the damage of the past, whether the hurt occurred years ago or a few minutes ago.

Notes

Chapter 4
The Key Steps in Forgiving

Inspiration and Motivation to Forgive

I believe that inspiration is the most important thing a person can have to succeed in anything—not money, not status but the motivation that comes from being truly inspired to do something. Of course, money, etc., can help in some endeavors, but deep inspiration is a great source of motivation. That is why I stress first of all to find your inspiration to forgive. The stronger the motivation, the greater the likelihood of success.

Molding one's life after an important inspirational person can carry you through great misfortunes and very difficult situations that need forgiving. Here is an example. During the apartheid violence in South Africa in 1993, a young black man killed Amy Biehls, an American Rhodes Scholar and exchange student. Her parents came from the U.S., met the young man's family, and decided to testify in court on his behalf so that he would receive a pardon. They said they could only do this because they knew it would be what their daughter would want.[1]

Many people in the world use a Divine figure of their religion.

Without being inspired in some way, the motivation to forgive might not be enough to deal with difficult situations that need forgiving.

Through the years that I had PTSD, I never tried to forgive the many upsets I had with people. Thus, since I had tried everything else and none worked, I felt convinced that forgiveness of all of my upsets with anyone would bring back the experience of Love and Joy I had earlier in my life. From childhood into my early twenties, I often experienced compassion, love, and joy.

My absolute intention to again feel that level of Love and Joy inspired me and gave me the willingness to let go of every upset I had. I wanted that goal more than holding onto any upset. I was convinced that those upsets prevented me from experiencing Divine Unconditional Love.

I was right. That inspiration carried me in one day through forgiving of the over 900 upsets. The result was Love filling me. It has remained with me all these years, as long as I hold not one resentment or upset with anyone, place, or thing. That is not easy. But having a sense of Love and Joy in my life keeps me working on letting go of whatever resentment or judgment I might hold. I have always been able to regain that beautiful sense using the tools in this book.

A person or child will not forgive just because you tell them they should. They must first be willing to forgive. The question then is, what will motivate the person to forgive? An adult might have poor health, depression, loss of a marriage or job or family, they want to get over. Forgiveness of recent and past upsets could just be the action that could change their life.

Here is some journal work you can do.
1. What is the highest goal that you have for yourself, your life, and your relationships?

2. Write down all the things you want to achieve.

3. Who or what would inspire you to let go of your upsets to get what you want?

If you are willing to forgive, you'll be open to the processes and questions outlined in this book. Your happiness rests squarely upon your willingness to do this work.

A Contract

Once you agree to do this work, Dr. Everett Worthington found that writing a contract of intention helps in the process.[2] I must admit I didn't do this with my own upsets for years. Then I read marketing research about gaining commitments. It showed that when a person signs a contract, they are more likely to stay with what they agreed to as opposed to those who did not sign a contract.[3]

Here is a sample contract that you can use or vary in any way that you want. You can put it in the journal or do it on a separate page.

By signing this contract, you are stating your promise to work on practicing the methods of forgiving yourself and others and being happier. This contract by Dr. Worthington is simply a sincere statement to give forgiveness a strong effort.[4]

Forgiveness Contract

I promise to myself and the person helping me (or that I am helping) that on _____, 20 ____, that I intend to do my best to use the exercises which we talk about and go over to try to forgive myself for things I've done to others that I don't feel good about and for the things others have done to me that upset me.

_____Signature
_____Date _____ Witness

You can vary the contract by changing the contract after the date to say:
I intend to try to forgive_____(name)
or myself for_____.

The Simplest Forgiveness Method: "I forgive."

Once you have the incentive to forgive and the signed contract(see p.   for an example), try this method; this originally came from a friend, Rosie Rodriguez, in Santa Rosa, California, who taught people to use a set of 490 forgiveness beads. The beads come from the question to Jesus on how many times we are to forgive. His answer was 70x7. It is simple, yet it works!

1. Think of a person you are upset with.
2. Say, "I forgive."
3. Do this over and over. After each 10 to 15 repetitions, think of something you are grateful for.
4. At some point, you will feel a felt-shift I mentioned earlier. It's a change in attitude, a lightening of spirit, a feeling of love, or new insight about the benefit of forgiving.

This simple method is effective for both small and large offenses and hurts.

Our Primary Needs

Understanding why negative things happen to us is necessary to predict how to be safer the next time and figure out what we can change.[5, 6] We like to have our situations neatly dealt with somehow so that they do not continually bother us by worrying or feeling hurt and insecure.[7] Unforgiveness, whether it is about our self or another, does not remedy a situation but allows it to fester in our minds.

Exercise on Getting Needs and Wants Met

Have you been unable to forgive because your point of view was ignored?

Write down what happened.

1. How did you feel?

2. Take a step back and look again at the other person involved in the upset. Did he or she feel satisfied with the outcome? Or is that person still upset as well?

3. How does insisting on a need or a want being met cause you to hold onto anger, resentment, and hostility?

4. Is hold onto anger, resentment, and hostility worth it? Write down what you can do to change your viewpoint in order to forgive.

The Awareness of Feelings

Through years of doing this work, I've found that the awareness of emotions makes a big difference. It is only one aspect of mindfulness.

When I worked with men in domestic violence counseling, accurately assessing emotions was always an essential part of their gaining control over an upset. Some of the men were astounded that we had so many feelings that they were not taught. To assist in an in-depth understanding of most emotions, I've provided a list of feelings in Appendix A. There are 80 negative ones on the list and 52 positive ones.

In anger control groups I ran at a Juvenile Detention Center in California, we started each session by giving the teens a list of feelings and then asked them what they were feeling. They always said the list helped. In some classes, I have used emoticon faces I found on the web to show the emotions.

You will need to be aware of your feelings, which will help deal with the upset.[8] We all need to learn coping skills and social-emotional skills to understand our emotions so that we are not be overwhelmed and controlled by them.[9]

In working with upsets, to say, "I'm angry!" is often not enough. Remembering upsets revive strong feelings. Anger is typical and easy for people to notice. Avoiding intense emotions is normal. However, it takes seeing the whole situation, including all the feelings that were pushed away, to forgive genuinely. I've found that feelings are a good entry point for forgiving. Often by accurately identifying the emotion, you can understand the whole situation better. In one example, a man named Jared was often angry. Each time he looked over the feeling list we had given him, he realized that he was humiliated instead of angry. Just finding that emotion helped alleviate his upsets and enabled him to forgive the situation more easily.

Feelings occur in layers, particularly anger. Anger can start as mild irritation and grow into unbridled fury.[10] Fear and grief can also drive anger. Have you experienced this? Or something like it?

Hopeless feelings contribute to depression and can cause ill health, mentally and physically.[11] Sometimes, just thinking of the upset and accurately identifying the underlying emotion can change the whole situation. In some classes, I have used emoticon faces I found on the web to show emotions.

When I taught anger control groups in Domestic Violence, accurately assessing emotions was always an essential part of gaining control over an upset.

In my experience, not all people can see the effect of their thoughts and feeling, thus see no reason to forgive. So, expecting others to forgive might be unrealistic.

Unrealistic Expectations

I've found that unforgiveness (unforgiven resentments, anger, and upsets) is simply an unrealistic expectation. That's it. Life provided something that you did not like, so you resisted it and wanted something different. The reason what was wanted is unrealistic is because it did not happen. What's real is what happened. In the 12-steps, they say, "Life on life's terms."

Forgiving is dealing with the situation that life has given instead of resisting, fighting, or regretting it. Someone did something you did not like. You had an unrealistic expectation that it should have played out differently. But it didn't, that's the reality. You are probably be right; it should not have happened. But it did. How do you deal with your disappointment or pain instead of still expecting something different?

Journal exercise

You can ask:

- What has life given me that is not right and that I would like to change? Write down those disagreements with life.

- What do you get by holding onto the upset?

- Can you let it go, or is there someone you need to forgive?

Remember, you can forgive and decide that the offender is not someone you want in your life. That is your decision. But wherever anger rears its head, unforgiveness is not far behind.

A Helpful Tool - Create a Detailed Analysis of the Upset

As I previously mentioned, many upsets are too tough to let go of with a simple gesture or conversation because we often experience strong emotions resulting from disappointments and setbacks. Frequently, we focus so much on the perceived injury that we lose track of how we might have contributed to the situation.

Now that you have the basics of forgiveness, here is a tool created by Dr. Eric Donaldson to look at people and situations to help you forgive. It is something basic you can work with right now and then build upon it.

Here is a workable format:

1. <u>Describe the upset.</u>

2. <u>What feelings are associated with it?</u>

3. <u>What is my inspiration?</u>

4. <u>Am I willing to work on it?</u>

5. <u>What debt am I owed?</u>

6. <u>What do I get from this the way it is now?</u>

7. <u>Can I forgive this?</u>

Example of a response:

1. <u>Describe the upset</u>: My Dad recently moved from Montana to Pennsylvania without telling me that he was moving. He does not have a phone, and he has made no effort to call me. It has been over two months, and I am worried about him.

2. <u>Feelings associated with it</u>: I am feeling hurt that he would not tell me; sad that we are out of touch; and angry that he is so stub

3. <u>What is my inspiration?</u> To have better communications with my Dad. To feel like I can connect with him.

4. <u>Am I willing to work on it?</u> Yes, I have learned that the lack of communication can impact loved ones directly. I am willing to look at this.

5. <u>What debt am I owed?</u> Knowing that my elderly father is alright. The decency of being told what someone I love is planning to do.

6. <u>What do I get from this the way it is now?</u> I feel justified in not attempting to contact him because I am hurt that he didn't tell me that he moved.

   The right to complain about him.

7. <u>Can I forgive this?</u> Yes. I am willing to forgive it, so long as we can work out a way to be in touch.

You can make a form like the above to answer those questions.

Notes

Chapter 5
Dealing with and Forgiving Yourself

Nurturing Yourself

Children and animals who are nurtured live with much less fear and stress. Nurturing creates protective chemicals around the cared-for person's DNA. Stress and lack of feeling safe and secure cause harm biologically.[1]

As you see, taking care of yourself is urgent. If you weren't nurtured well by your parents, you can change that by doing that now by continuing this work.

Gratitude

One way to nurture yourself, which also helps in forgiving, is through gratitude, being thankful. Many individuals and groups around the world have found that practicing gratitude every day truly brings about miracles.

A Positive Psychology research team found that one of the most effective ways to have happiness was to use gratitude daily. In the study, people wrote down three good things, big or small, that happened during the day. They did this every night for one week. Next to each entry, they answered the question, "Why did this good thing happen?" After three months, these people were still significantly happier and less depressed than the control group.[2]

Journal Exercise

1. Write down things for which you are grateful.

2. Next to each one, ask: "What brought about this good thing?

Gratitude is also an extremely powerful way to shift a negative perspective. In an experiment on gratitude and well-being in daily life, one research group reported that those who were grateful had:

- more positive feelings and fewer negative ones
- less physical pain
- more hours of sleep and awoke more refreshed
- less focus on hassles or complaints
- more positive and optimistic appraisals of one's life
- more energy for exercising, and
- fewer reported physical symptoms.[3]

Research at the University of California, Los Angeles, Mindfulness Awareness Research Center showed that an attitude of gratitude changes the brain's molecular structure, making us healthier and happier, more peaceful, less reactive, and less resistant.[4]

In a study at the University of California, Berkeley, participants who wrote one letter of gratitude each week for three weeks reported much better mental health for up to 12 weeks after the writing exercise ended. They had significantly better results than those who wrote about negative experiences or who only received counseling.[5]

Finding the Metaphor

Understanding that the mind uses metaphors for thinking was essential for me to let go of most of my upsets.[6]

Metaphors are illustrations that make a strong point by comparing two things you wouldn't necessarily pair together; for example, "His words cut deeper than a knife." Here, words aren't sharp objects. In this metaphor, someone has said something hurtful to another[7] or the verse in a song, "You are the wind beneath my wings." The person doesn't have wings, but the wind and the wings symbolize the person's relationship to the other.

For example, when I was trying to forgive a mass murder, I had not killed anyone, but as I looked at what that stood for, I could see how I killed myself metaphorically. When I look at how someone is judgmental, I can see the metaphor of how it applies to me. Refusing to see how an unforgiven situation applies to me takes us deeper into how the mind works to defend us by blaming others for something we have done. This keeps the solution to healing hidden upsets. It is called scape-goating. In psychology, it's called projection.

Because our experiences and feelings are linked to earlier experiences of the same feelings,[8, 9] I try to help people find earlier experiences of the same feeling in forgiveness work. The experiences are not the same, but the feelings often are. If a person is trying to forgive someone for hurting their feelings, the earlier situation might be how the forgiver hurt people's feelings. That would be the projection so that they wouldn't feel guilty themselves.

When I work with a couple and things are not going well in forgiveness work, I ask if the spouse represents their father or mother. That usually reveals the source of the upset.

Sin

The original meaning of "sin" is from Greek meaning—**to miss the mark**. When you miss the mark, you keep trying to do well and keep practicing until you hit where you are aiming. Forgiveness through reevaluating unrealistic expectations and focusing on valuable targets is the key to attaining what you want. The only point of missing the mark is to gain better skills.

Try this to find out how others influence your decision to forgive by looking at family and friends' opinions about a situation you find difficult. Addressing the following questions will allow you to go deeper into the social and cultural assumptions that keep you from forgiving.

1. What are people close to you saying that prevents you from forgiving? Write it down.

2. What will people think of you if you forgive? Write down the names that come up and what they may say to you or each other.

3. Are there any unwritten rules that people believe about what you are dealing with?

Guilt, Pain, Punishment, and Self-conflict

Through the years, I've seen when people who have done something they feel very guilty about will often find ways to punish themselves. Sometimes they will do it through using drugs, alcohol, risky behavior, etc., even illness.

Our values, rules, and moral code set the standard for how we live. When we act against our values, we feel bad and may also experience a sense of guilt. Our perceived lack of worthiness keeps us from our inner peace and power. Guilt can often make us think we deserve punishment.

This constant loop of negative emotions and thoughts is destructive and can keep someone depressed and feeling the world is against them.

In his book, *Big Prisons, Big Dreams: Crime and the Failure of America's Penal System*, Michael J. Lynch goes over the three methods for changing behavior: positive reinforcement, negative reinforcement, and punishment. He shows how **punishment is the least effective on humans**. Positive reinforcement is the most successful.[10] Please take this to heart when dealing with yourself and others.

Punishing yourself is not useful in changing behavior for the better.[11] Punishment has been used for eons in cultures to change behavior. Through habit, we will usually do what was done to us. Nevertheless, resist this temptation for self-punishment because it results in fear by activating fight and flight increasing resentment. Since you are trying to avoid resentment, this defeats your purpose in self-forgiving.

Only when we recognize the conflicts we have with ourselves can we look deeper and forgive ourselves. Research has found that guilt helps us to forgive because it keeps us humble.[12]

However, that doesn't mean their feelings of guilt will enable them to forgive themself to end their internal pain. It might take a major change in attitude or personality. Who is to say? However, I know from experience those who work on their character defects—as they say in the 12 steps—and recognize the conflicts they have with themselves. Working on cleaning those up can change their situation. Forgiveness helps along the way.

The Keys to Self-Forgiveness are:

♦ Facing your wrongs done

♦ Replacing them with compassion, generosity, and love.

Self-forgiveness happens when there are positive feelings, actions, and thoughts for one's self. You are gaining that skill here.

The Cycle of Victimhood and Guilt

Here is how it goes I've found:

We do something against our moral codes, rules, or values. → This leads to guilt, shame, regret. → We then condemn ourselves, and thus, → we accept punishment from ourselves or others because we feel we deserve it. → Our self-protective defenses kick in, and then → we blame others for what happened. → We attack them, subtly or overtly, thus creating more guilt for ourselves. →We also fear attack from them, which often justifies attacking them more, which keeps the whole cycle going.

Forgiveness can enter this cycle at any point and change it.

1.   Have you seen this in your life when you have felt guilty?

2.   Did things go well in your life?

3.   Did life seem to be against you when you hurt people?

4.   How can forgiving yourself and others make this situation better?

Giving and Receiving

If you can identify what prevents you from having love, you could have more of it. This is also true of joy, peace, and other positive feelings. Love takes a back seat when we choose to resent, to be angry, or to hate. In some way, you receive what you give. If you are angry, realistically, that is what you are giving, and you get the result. Anger gets results, but are those results worth the cost?

The Beatles said it very nicely in the song, The End: "The love you take is equal to the love you make."

Journal Entry

1.   If you feel that you are not getting the positives from life that you deserve, look more deeply at your worthiness, which is in your eyes only.

2. As self-forgiveness is the key to inner riches and worth, search out any unworthy feelings.

3. Find the guilt associated with unworthiness. It's there.

Gaining Self-Forgiveness

You cannot always forgive yourself just by trying, but you can regain forgiveness by doing something that would bring about your forgiveness in your own heart. Sometimes you need to make amends for what you did, as they do in the 12-step programs. Or, you might need to turn to a Higher Power for help in releasing your heart from self-torment.

Self-torment is often misplaced because it was, perhaps, the result of a fight-flight reaction that overrode your rational thinking. In that case, an act to help gain self-forgiveness would be to learn how to control those reactions effectively.

Researchers have shown that our survival mechanisms are fully engaged right after birth.[13] As we get older, we continue to use more of them for protection and well-being.

We regain strength and power that un-forgiveness takes from us when we show compassion for another's situation, as well as our own, and forgive them and ourselves.

1. Look at acts you did wrong or did not do well that you still feel bad about. Write them down.

2. Have your actions hurt another or others? If so, write down those people's names in your journal. Write down how your wrong-doing may have hurt each one.

3. Now, look at what caused you to act that way. Was it because you disliked someone? Have you blamed someone for a wrong done to you? Just what was it?

4. Write your justification for acting that way?

5. Have you used this justification before? If so, in what situations? Is the problem always the same? Write down what you find.

6. Contemplate what it would take for you to change that behavior. Take your time. Write down what you find. What do you need? Can you forgive yourself? Do you need to ask for inner intuitive help or make amends?

Earning Forgiveness from Others

Sometimes we need to receive forgiveness from those we have hurt to feel right about ourselves. To obtain forgiveness often takes at least an apology. In her book, The Power of Apology, Beverly Engel gives us a useful three-step method for providing a meaningful apology:

1. State your regret for causing the situation.
2. Accept responsibility for what you did.
3. Give the person a way to repair the harm done, perhaps a pledge or act.[14]

Her book gives plenty of helpful ideas on doing these steps.

Research shows that, when done truthfully, an apology can easily lead the victim to see that the offender is experiencing guilt and emotional distress for how the hurtful actions harmed the victim. This honest and sincere apology can lead to empathy for the offender and a better possibility of reconciliation.[15]

Age and maturity can also affect our judgment of ourselves. I've seen many times that we judge ourselves by our standards and age now, forgetting the lack of wisdom and maturity we had when the situation occurred or the impact of a lower brain takeover.

1. With each self-unforgiveness, look at what you did from the perspective of your age and maturity at the time.

2. Is it still realistic to judge yourself, given who you were at the time?

Empowering Yourself and Others

Connecting with a higher aspect of life is the best way to empower yourself. For some, this seems difficult. I created Effective Ways of Empowering Yourself and Others for my workshops and classes to enable people to work with many of their inner strength sources available to us all. These have helped many clients and students connect with the power they required to forgive. See Appendix B for questions to help you.

Notes

Chapter 6
More Tools for Letting Go of Upsets

How to deal with stress is a crucial tool in forgiving. We will address it in this chapter and the next one.

Our Stress Responses

Offenses activate our fight, flight, freeze, and flock brain reactions.[1] These reactions are part of our Sympathetic Nervous System (SNS), which is for our protection and prepares the body for stressful or emergency situations. Its counterpart is the Parasympathetic Nervous System (PSNS), which is set up to control body processes during ordinary conditions. It is for conserving and restoring our energy. It slows the heart rate and decreases blood pressure.[2] The PSNS helps us adapt and cope with stress. It is increased by forgiveness and diminished by unforgiveness.[3]

When an upset occurs, we are gripped with fear, anger, feeling overwhelmed, etc. Facing our most painful situations often feels as though it will kill us. But running from these "demons" gives them power. Those intense emotions and reactions keep our stress system, our sympathetic (fight and flight) nervous system, going, not only preventing forgiveness but also sapping our joy of living.

Many unforgiven, unresolved events can leave your mind in a negative state much of the time. I was well aware of this in my own life. Avoiding the memory of an upset is not in your best interest because the hurt or guilt remains under the surface of awareness, negatively coloring life.[4]

A better life demands that we step out of our overwhelming emotions. Some people use food, work, sex, drugs, alcohol, etc., to silence the fear and pain. All are inadequate and temporary fixes.

Quieting the Stress Reactions

Under stress, rationality is outweighed by strong emotions and impulses, causing us to consider "pathological" behavior, such as suicide, violence, shooting sprees, terrorism, and war. Forgiving helps quiet the fearful mind but is difficult when the stress responses are actively in control. You regain control by finding a safe place in your thoughts and environment.

Good examples for calming the mind are meditation, prayer, going to a church, listening to soothing music, contemplation, being in nature, massage, yoga, exercise, reading something inspirational, taking a shower, exercising, talking with friends, etc. Do as many as possible.

Stress is a part of growing up in a complex and confusing world of fears, pressures, school and family issues, learning challenges, competition, friendships, and achieving goals. Though we would like to protect ourselves from stress, worries, and anxiety, it is not practical nor helpful in the long run. Pressures, challenges, and fear are part of life. For example, trees grown in enclosed spaces where there's no wind end up being much weaker and can't survive for long. Stress is what makes a tree strong enough to sustain the wear and tear that it'd face later in life.[5]

The best way to shield yourself from the harmful effects of stress is to learn scientifically backed and easy-to-do stress management methods.[6]

The Best Stress Management Method

There is plenty of research concerning forgiveness and how it aids in effectively dealing with stress. Dr. Loren Toussaint, a renowned forgiveness researcher, ran a study that proved increases in forgiveness were associated with decreases in stress, which were related to reductions in mental health symptoms.[7] As far back as 2004, Everett Worthington, another well-respected forgiveness researcher, did a complete analysis of forgiveness research and stress, including the chemical pathways showing how valuable forgiveness is for combatting stress.[8]

It's only logical that this would be so. Forgiveness removes many of the stressors from the mind as opposed to merely trying to quiet them down. Thus, the mind has fewer stressors to contend with. This benefit includes situations when a person is upset with themselves or with others.

Results of stress-monitoring research done on people showed that having a person think about forgiving (just thinking, not doing) brought down the person's stress levels.[9]

Forgiveness is powerful in dealing with stress, but ironically, to forgive, you need to reduce stress to defuse the fight and flight mechanism. To calm it down more quickly, learn the two effective stress management methods below.

The Relaxation Response Method

Important Note: It takes only 20 minutes to notice a dramatic shift away from the stressed brain-reactivity if you do something to calm it down. Attempting nothing gets you nothing.

Noted researcher, Herbert Benson M.D., called this method "the relaxation response," making it well-known in the 1980s. It is simply having the person *say a significant word (such as peace, love, joy, etc.) on each out-breath for 20 minutes.*

Some use the name of a religious figure or loved one.

The relaxation response time can be lowered to 5 minutes by practicing it regularly every day for 20 minutes.[10] You can look up the full method online, but the above steps sum up most of what you need to know.

One of the falsehoods about forgiving that people use not to forgive is: I'm just too angry! Or too hurt to forgive. If you find you are feeling too upset to do forgiveness work, first do the Relaxation Response to calm down. This is a crucial time to work deeply. This is where stress reduction methods help.

The Orange Juice Relaxation Method

I've successfully used this method with all age groups.

♦ Picture filling your body with orange juice from the top of your head to the bottom of your feet.

♦ Now, be aware of your head and tensions, aches, pains, stiffness, or soreness you might have in your forehead, eyes, back of the neck, and jaws, and let the orange juice flow out of your head through your fingers, taking the aches and pains with it. Tell me when you have done that.

- Now, be aware of your neck and shoulders relaxing as the orange juice drains out of that area, removing the tensions, aches, pains, stiffness, or soreness out through your fingers.

- Do the same with anything you might feel in your arms. Let it go as the juice goes out your fingers.

- Be aware of your chest, back, and belly. Take your time letting go of whatever discomfort you feel in those areas as you visualize the orange juice flowing out your toes. Tell me when you have done that.

- Be aware of your lower belly, butt, and each leg. Let go of the tension or discomfort in those areas as the orange juice flows out your toes. Tell me when you have done that.

- Now check over your body to see if there are any areas where the orange juice got stuck and let go of the tensions, aches, pains, stiffness, or soreness in those areas. Tell me when you've done that.

The idea of doing this relaxation exercise is consistency. You don't have to stick to the script after a while. Play with it, make it fun.

A relaxation of this sort is usually done before any guided visualization so that tensions are out of the way to do more in-depth work.

Betrayal, Safety, and Trust

Through my years of hearing about people's resentments, it seems that betrayal is behind much of our unforgiveness. Being betrayed can radically change our perspective about our safety in our lives.

We expect actions against us from our enemy. That is what an enemy is – someone we cannot trust and, indeed, isn't safe to be with or nurturing. Betrayal comes from someone we trust, someone we have faith in to honor and respect us. Then, suddenly—their world view is disturbed drastically. Suddenly, the world becomes unsafe, and as a result, even life or God can become untrustworthy.

As we have talked of, without a sense of safety, the fight and flight mechanism is always engaged, preventing clear thinking and especially joy because the person is on edge. Only in a safe environment can our brain's fight-and-flight mechanism relax, allowing our parasympathetic nervous system to take control to relax the muscles and slow the heart.

The death of a loved one can throw us into chaos because our safety in some way depended on their connection to us, especially if it was nurturing. Often, we need to forgive the person who died because they "abandoned" us. This is not something to be ashamed of feeling; it is natural. They took away safety and nurturing when they died.

When someone or organization in which we have faith does something to violate our rules or codes for behavior, like cheating on us with someone else, stealing our money, or intentionally hurting us, that can destroy our sense of safety and trust. These hurts might even affect our sense of self and who we are. Cults and abusers do this intentionally so that the person lets go of family, friends, and who they depend on so that they can be remolded into who the abuser wants them to be. What happens is called Trauma Bonding or Betrayal Bonding.[10a]

This intentional violation of our codes or safety means forgiving must reach a deeper level. In Trauma-Informed Care and PTSD situations, I know that many drift into a sense of low self-esteem, depression, or isolation. Life itself can seem unsafe, uncertain, not worth living, a view that many have who have been betrayed. Since that is often the case, the betrayed person needs to rebuild their sense of safety.

Even love can have a double edge. When we love a person, place, or thing, they can also betray us by changing in ways we did not expect. We can love our bodies, and they can betray us by aging, getting a disease, or having other problems we cannot rectify. Even our society and politics can betray us, for change seems to be the only constant in life. Forgiveness will bring a sense of safety for you because your stressed nervous system will be far less activated.

In order to achieve a deep, foundational sense of safety, I had to forgive everything. I had to rebuild **me** on stronger ground that could not be disturbed by someone or something else's action. Only five times in 27 years was my sense of Love and security undone. When I forgave in those instances, Love and Joy came back. Each forgiveness was a blessing that made me stronger in my conviction of where to build my trust.

I trust Love because I always know how to access it. If Love is not present in my heart, I find who or what I have not forgiven or have judged. Then it returns. It's not in another's hands to betray me.

There seem to be two forces in the world—the force for good and for evil. There are many symbols for this in every culture. God and the devil are an obvious example. Not only is this opposition in our world, but it is also within us. The typical example is the angel on one shoulder and the devil on the other, or the ego vs. the higher self. Betrayal brings the negative voice to the forefront, and it often takes over—the result, depression, grief, anger.

How can you trust someone who does not give you a sense of safety in your world? Your sense of security must be built on more than a person, place, thing, or organization. By forgiving every upset in your life, you naturally gain a sense of safety because your mind becomes more relaxed. This enables your brain's "executive functions," which are involved in critical thinking, problem-solving, planning, reasoning, and decision making;[11] and forgiving,[12] to be in control.

Exercise:
If you have been betrayed, try this:

1. How did the person's actions take away your sense of safety?

2. What is the rule or code that they broke?

3. Is that rule or code something that you always, in every instance, live by? Is the rule or code true in all instances?

4. Do you want to build trust with that person again?

5. If so, forgiveness is a good first step, but trust and feeling safe will take time, negotiation, and setting limits on bad behavior.

6. If not, can you forgive anyway, which does not mean reconciling with them? It only means you feeling better.

Personal Responsibility Exercise

- Do I want to keep this situation alive?

- Even if "they" seem to be the sole cause of the problem, how might I be keeping it going?

- Is my logic getting in the way of the right thing to do in this situation?

- Are my emotions getting in the way of the right thing to do in this situation?

- Am I turning people to side with me to justify my position?

- What was my part in all of this? Did I make it worse?

- How can I take care of myself better?

Building A Sense of Trust In A Family or Organization

Researchers from the business schools at the University of Chicago, the University of Pennsylvania, and Carnegie Mellon set up models to predict trustworthy behaviors and intentions. They found that participants who signed the code of conduct were much more likely to be reliable and suggest that reminding employees of the importance of responsibility and making codes of conduct prominent may help create a trustworthiness culture.[13]

In the world today of false data and lying, perhaps with this knowledge of trustworthiness, an admirable way to build trust, accountability, and responsibility in a family or business is to have a written and agreed-upon code of conduct.[14] It obviously won't deal with every situation but can help.

Help from Another Level of The Mind and Heart

For me (and the people I have worked with), help comes from our intuition when there is intention toward forgiving and peace. There are many names for that intuitive help, the Voice, the Holy Spirit, Inner Guidance, Higher Self, Guardian Angel, the right brain, etc. The name doesn't matter. That there is inner help does matter when we put our full willingness and intention into forgiving.

Each time you look more deeply into your mind and heart, you further develop the skill to uncover upsets instead of hiding them away.

Exercise in Asking for Inner Help or Intuition

In difficult situations, inner resources such as intuition, hunches, insight, and inner guidance can be beneficial in the practice of forgiveness. Accessing intuition requires that you maintain an open mind and a willingness to receive new possibilities.

1. Have you ever had a hunch about something? Or an insight?

2. Did this new truth help you deal with a person, a situation, or a problem?

3. Did you use this new truth in your life? If yes, great. If not, what got in the way?

Through the years, I've seen people who pray or ask for inner help in forgiving receive it. Deep inner help or intuition is often available. A simple request that has worked for me many times is, "Please help me to see this in a different way." I cannot tell you how the help will manifest or how it will benefit specifically, but I know that it will come and assist the person who asks. That is the way I got through my immense forgiveness list.

Here is an exercise to assist in connecting to inner help available to us all.

1. Relax and think about the highest in yourself as you do your forgiveness work.

2. Take a moment now to ask for inner help to assist you in forgiving. Ask for help to see your situation in a new light.

3. Whenever you bog down in your forgiveness work, close your eyes, become silent, and make a sincere request for help

4. When you have done all you can, let the struggle go and listen.

Notes

Chapter 7
What's Behind Your Thoughts and Feelings?

To help me better understand forgiveness and the mechanisms that prevent it, I've studied the brain for almost twenty years. As far back as the 1800s, scientists were examining the unconscious/subconscious motivations that affect our behavior.

Through the years, my students have very much appreciated learning more about the brain and how it affects our behavior, thinking, and forgiveness. Learning about these interactions can be calming because knowledge empowers us.

Today we are aware of the brain's many alarm circuits and defense systems critical to our survival that function below our conscious awareness. These alarm circuits include a) nursing and protection of offspring and family, and b) activities like friendship, love and affection, laughter and playfulness, and control of aggressive behaviors. In fact, researchers consider that these mechanisms steer the consciousness of all of us. [1]

Our brain evolved to protect us. To pass on our genes to the next generation, humans had to live long enough to mate, which meant we had to survive at least 15-20 years. With current life expectancies above 70 years, that drive is not as essential to species survival as it was before. But, just a hundred years ago, life was not so easy, and the centuries before that were even more challenging. As a result, the brain evolved to be fine-tuned for detecting anything harmful because it meant DANGER! Neuropsychology Researcher Dr. Rick Hanson describes it beautifully in his books and YouTube videos. [2,3]

Fortunately, through the ages, we have evolved brain structures that contribute to higher brain functions and emotions, like compassion, empathy, forgiveness, love, and altruism. We can call upon these higher functions to override the more primitive fight-and-flight reactions. In many ways, forgiveness helps us to overcome our stressed brain responses. If you can see a hurt or upset from a higher perspective or a calmer point of view, it is often much easier to let it go.[4] For example, one of our contributors to the book wrote:

"During my commute each day, I encounter many types of drivers, and for the most part, I focus being the cooperative type of driver. I have noticed, however, that there is a certain type of driver that I have a hard time with. He is the CHEATER. You know this individual--he's the one who will run you off the road to get one car length ahead. Whenever I encounter this person, my first reaction is competition. I want to do whatever I can to thwart his cheating. My next response is a strong desire to retaliate, to make him suffer. These are strong urges, driven by a tit-for-tat mentality, competition, and a desire to punish the cheater by seeking revenge. Fortunately, most of the time (sadly, not all), I am able to catch myself in the midst of this lower brain tantrum, halting this urge by calling on compassion and empathy. I do this by imagining that the other driver is in a hurry to see his daughter's performance or to visit a sick relative instead of focusing on the perceived attack on me and my space. In this manner, I'm able to let it go and calm down so that I can be a safer driver myself."

Thoughts and Emotions

Your thoughts do not emerge independently per incident. Instead, they are fully integrated with previously formed nerve pathways on those subjects.[5] For example, riding a bike is linked to the experience of walking and balance. Thus, each person takes in his or her new experience differently. Future problems begin when our brains link even pleasurable experiences with episodes of stress.[5a]

The parts of the brain that have to do with emotions bring interest, passion, and the ability to nurture, love, and protect our families and friends. They also cause and control our aggressive behaviors.[6]

"Emotion is the messenger of love," Psychiatrists Lewis, Amini, and Landon tell us in *A General Theory of Love*. They add that emotions carry the signals of our heart to one another and that, for many of us, feeling deeply is the experience of being alive.[6a]

This sounds good, doesn't it? The problem occurs when we withdraw love, usually due to rejection or betrayal from others. Then other strong emotions like misery or rage, to name a couple, can take hold and cause terrible consequences in our mind and body.

When negative thoughts dominate our consciousness, they can cause moodiness, irritability, clinical depression, increasingly pessimistic thinking and perceptions, and decreased or excess motivation/drive. They can also lead to floods of undesirable emotions, appetite and sleep problems, decreased sexual responsiveness, social isolation, sadness, and hopelessness.[9] This is especially true for children because their brains are not fully formed to deal with that level of stress.

Though there is controversy among neuroscientists about which brain structures influence our emotions, our focus regarding forgiveness is the fear mechanism and the structures that activate fear reactions.[10] Since many of our responses have to do with fear and its link to unconscious survival defenses, fear is the area I've found to be most fruitful to work with in forgiving. Asking others or myself, "what do you or did you fear in your unforgiven event?" always gives significant insight and understanding about the incident.

In stress and emotional turmoil, our control of aggressive behavior decreases. Anger, revenge, and jealousy can increase, even leading to a shutdown or rational thought processes. In legal terms, this is *temporary insanity,* and in laymen's terms, *crimes of passion.*

Neuroscience research clearly shows that stress can affect brain development. Calming stress can significantly improve well-being and the ability to forgive. These next sections will explain how.

The Neocortex

Most people are familiar with this part of the brain. It is said to be the highest functioning part of our brain,[9] takes up the most space in our heads, and is the primary storehouse of our information and memories. It:

♦ Performs higher functions such as sensory perception, generation of motor commands, spatial reasoning, conscious thought, and in humans, language. [10]

♦ Generates our ideas, gives us our capacity for concentration, and uses symbols to produce our ability to read, write, talk, and do math. [11]

♦ Helps us to be not only logical and systematic but also intuitive and imaginative. [12]

♦ Rejects and suppresses unacceptable social responses. [13]

♦ Coordinates with other parts of the brains – enabling us to have empathy and better judgment.[14]

The Prefrontal Lobes

Forgiveness comes from the prefrontal lobes of the neocortex, which are behind our forehead.[15] Our "executive functions" also come from this area, i.e., planning, organizing, remembering details, making decisions, and solving problems.[15a] The prefrontal lobes control negative emotions and support our positive emotions, like compassion, empathy, love, and altruism.[15b, 15c]

You can see that using our neocortex more of the time would have positive outcomes. However, in threatening situations or when we experience hopelessness, our fight-and-flight brain systems can shut down our neocortex. This shutdown is for our survival but has many adverse effects if the stress goes too long.[16]

The Earliest Parts of our Brain

Learning about this section on the brain can help understand your possible reactions to upsets. In the center of our brains are some of our earliest and most established parts, for example, our "emotional neural networks" that determine how we react to events.[17] These earlier parts are adaptations that shaped our brains and helped us develop unconscious modes of operation to more easily deal with the problems humans have encountered since the days of our very early ancestors.[17a] They are responsible for survival and quick action, like protecting offspring[17b] and especially adaptations that affected reproduction.[17c]. They are the foundation of our physical and species survival. [17d]

Basically, we have two modes for dealing with information— (a) autopilot and (b) conscious action. Our auto-pilot or automatic processing—learned over many generations, handles some of the universal features of our general social world and environment. Only with effort and mindfulness can we override our ancient automatic adaptations to tackle new challenges. This involves our consciously controlled problem-solving, enabling us to deal with differences and problems in our surroundings, especially to anticipate future changes and come up with viable coping strategies.[18a.]

Thus, though we have these predispositions from our ancestral inheritance, we can control their detrimental effects. For example, fear or dislike of foreigners, which may have come from an early ancestral protective adaptation, can be overcome by thinking rationally about it and by seeking contacts with those different from us.[18c]

Here are some of the basic survival adaptations and brain networks that affect:

• **Control of territory** – Our space is our empire, our territory. Here is the source of reactions, especially fear, to strangers or people who are different. This starting place of prejudice comes out of our basic need to protect what is ours.[19] Under stress, it becomes "I will attack any stranger who enters my space." In driving, we see this manifest as road rage, which often results from a violation of one's space or "territory." In your life, you might be overly touchy about your "space" and things.[20]

• **Establishing who is in and who is out** – is a subset of territorial control. It can happen early and is in all of us. What is like me is in, not like me is out. This is one of the bases of racism.[21] Everyone has it to some degree, some more than others, depending on how they are raised. A researcher working with preschool kids gave them either a green or orange shirt, with no difference in the shirts. The kids were then asked about the quality of the person in the pictures they were shown. The children favored the pictures of kids who wore their color of shirt, with no other difference than the shirt's color. This is called ingroup bias.[21a]

• **Courting and mating behavior and displays** – These actions guarantee the survival of the species. This area includes sexual aggression and submission. Here lie the answers to why a girl or woman sometimes submits against her better judgment to sexual aggression, and why girls and boys may become overwhelmed with sexual desires lies in this area.[22]

• **Control of interaction with others** – This is the drive for social maintenance and dominance by establishing a pecking order and command chain. At the deepest level, we are social beings. Here is why we tend to follow the crowd and its standards and have awe for authority.[23]

• **Ritual behavior** – Even infants are born with the ability to detect and imitate rituals. Some researchers say we're born ready to ritualize our life. When anxiety and stress overwhelm us, rituals reinstate our control.[24] Following regular rituals and having ceremonies is valuable in keeping people part of the social matrix and having them feel included as part of the group.[25] Thus, routines and patterns give us a basic sense of security and belonging.[26] This is why we organize. Here is the force behind religions, governments, and institutions.[27] Under stress, these rituals and activities may become compulsions--the person becomes obsessed with doing them.[28]

These levels of our older brain structures usually keep our social and group interactions at a priority. At their highest influence, they are the motivation for forgiveness; at their lowest is violence and fascism. Out of this desire for social interaction and control comes imitating, copying, and deception—all to be part of the group. The fashion industry is built on this drive. [29]

Change in any of the above areas can bring about strong reactions. Fear drives the reactive responses. It produces our basic fear reflex, which manifests as aggression or submission. [30] This is why being bullied can be so devastating for a child and why some kids bully.

Through the years, I've seen that these primitive brain pathways are the main reason we resist forgiving. These pathways can easily become our enemy and sabotage us if we let them have control for too long. For example, a person walks up on stage and freezes, forgetting everything they were to say. These pathways don't incapacitate us to harm us but are just doing their survival job honed eons ago when we were hunter-gatherers. When threats are perceived, they cause a person to attack, be violent, run away, or withdraw. [31] They can make a person a victim. [32, 33]

Make no mistake about it—this is not you! It's normal for a person to misidentify these stressed-brain reactions as one's own. They're not. All mammals and many other animals have them. It's like calling a computer program the computer. The program might be faulty and cause trouble with the computer's functioning, but the program is not the computer. They are both quite different.

Any person's stressed brain reactions can be changed and repaired to function correctly. We fix them by learning to calm down that stressed defensive system. That is one of our essential parental and education functions that we often fail at—teaching our kids how to think clearly and act sensibly under the stress of family, school, and peers' performance demands. Those who can do it succeed in those areas. [34]

I have found that the Lovingkindness blessing works the best to get me to the other side of the stressed brain reactions. Those stressed reactions won't go away as they are a part of our biological protection; they just don't have control over us. Through the years, they have become a habit that requires breaking. I have found that the Lovingkindness blessing works the best to get me to the other side of the stressed brain reactions. Those stressed reactions won't go away as they are a part of our biological protection; they just don't have control over us. Through the years, they have become a habit that requires breaking.

THE STEPS TO TAKE FOR COMPLETE FORGIVENESS

We are a complex mixture of mind, body, emotions, and spiritual focus, not an ancient programmed protective reaction. When we misperceive ourselves or others as this program, we set ourselves up for unhappiness.

Exercise

Look at each of the areas below and journal about how you might be negatively influence by each.

1. Control of territory

2. Establishing who is in and who is out

3. Courting and mating behavior and displays

4. Control of interaction with others

5. Ritual behavior

The Brain as Protector

Please note that each of our brains usually is on our side, not the other person's side. Our minds distort what happened in a situation to our favor, making us right and the other wrong. It is normal for the brain to be self-referential, defensive, and self-protective. It will even deny the harmful acts we do and justify our perspective. That's what it does; it's a coping mechanism.[35]

Though an abused person would like an apology, that can often be unrealistic because the offender's defensiveness will often deny or minimize what happened.

Primates do the same thing. Somebody asked the famous Koko, the gorilla who learned sign language, about the sink that had just been torn out of the wall. He blamed his kitten friend, who he was holding in the palm of his hand.[36]

Learning and Habits

The brain is set up for learning. Learning is created by making many nerve connections in the brain. In the gray matter of the brain, there are about 86 billion nerve cells (neurons). Each one can make an average of 7,000 connections with other neurons.[37] Each connection is built on previous connections, so even before we are born, we learn about pleasure, pain, comfort, safety, etc., through mom's reactions.

When you learn something, your brain cells (neurons) create connections (pathways) to that subject. The more you learn about a topic, the stronger the neural pathway becomes, until there is a "superhighway of nerve cells" to that subject.[37a] This is a habit, which is why you can drive and not think about it.

The neurons also make connections to similar subjects,[37b] like learning to ride a bike is associated with balance and walking, and perhaps later with skating. The more it is done, the better the child is at it. My daughter's friend taught her how to do cartwheels when they were four years old. She did them all the time. At six, she learned to ride a bike within five tries. She loved gymnastics and learn ice skating quickly, and later dance competitions and performances. All of these she practiced a lot, I mean a lot! This enhanced her balance skill.

The problem with these neural pathways is that the nerve connections do not differentiate between good and destructive behaviors. The nerves simply make "learning" connections. Thus, people who continue to say negative things about themselves create stronger neural pathways to those negative thoughts until there is a superhighway to them, making the person feel more and more inferior.

Focusing on the Negative

To make things more challenging, the brain's survival mechanisms focus on the negative keeps us safe and alive. Their job is to keep us alert to danger. We are always scanning for danger and problems, even when we're safe.[38]

Situations where danger is ongoing keep the survival parts of the brain active creating stress. If there is no relief from overactive stress responses, there can be serious mental, emotional, and physical consequences.[39] The most obvious is the Post Traumatic Stress Disorder (PTSD) symptoms of combat veterans who have to stay hyper-vigilant to remain alive. However, PTSD can also happen to anyone under constant danger, like a child or mother in a domestic violence situation, living in poverty, or unsafe neighborhoods.

The problem with hyper-vigilance is that the stressed system does not relax once the danger is over because the system has been activated for so long. It can take years to de-escalate on its own. In the meantime, the person reacts to things that they consider dangerous when they aren't, including people close to them.[40]

This happens not just in combat veterans, but anywhere where a person has experienced trauma and abuse, such as in prison.

- Have you seen this in your life, or the life of people close to you?

If you harbor grudges and negative feelings for those who have hurt you, your brain is creating a superhighway of nerve connections to adapt to this chronic line of negative thinking. This habit of focusing on negative feelings or outcomes keeps your thoughts in a rut.

This rut is a consequence of "rumination," which is continuously recalling some bad experience or feeling. You won't be able to stop thinking this way unless you tackle it head-on by examining what lies underneath the thoughts and taking action to get out of the rut. The researchers found the best way to break the cycle is part of the forgiveness process. It's called "compassionate reappraisal," where the offender is considered a human being who behaved unjustly, and the victim genuinely wishes for the offender's positive transformation in response.[41] This is the work of forgiveness. For me, compassionate reappraisal helped relieve me of over 17 years of PTSD.

Please be aware that lots of rumination on revenge prevents us from coming up with positive memory toward a transgressor (forgiveness), which means you will need to explore reasons to get out of the desire for revenge. [42]

Exercise

The following two exercises are not easy but can give remarkable insights into your thought patterns.

Ask these questions or variations of them.

1. Look at what you predominantly think about and feel during the day. You don't have to dig deeply into this exercise.

2. Briefly journal what you find. The idea here is to start identifying your thinking and feeling habits and emotional patterns to resolve them.

Here is an exercise to help with the two actions above:
1. Carry a pad with you through the day, writing down your most frequent thinking/feeling habit(s). Take your time.

2. Write down the positive ones in column 1 and the negatives ones in column 2.

3. If you become aware of contradicting thoughts like 'I love my mom, but she often upsets me.' Write them both in their respective columns.

4. Write about how you feel about what you found.

Our Comfort Zone

Our comfort zone is not always the healthiest place for us, but it is the most familiar. For example, I've heard that some people who grew up in what is today a war zone return to their homes because of past thoughts of comfort and familiarity, even though the conditions there are dangerous. Familiarity with a place and its people doesn't necessarily equate with safety, and re-engaging with them may re-ignite upsets and negative behaviors associated with them. We often see this when an alcoholic or addict comes out of rehabilitation and goes back to his old friend and haunts.

Here is an exercise to do.

1. Look at the places where you are most comfortable, the people you feel safest with, and the situations that make you feel at peace, safe, and in control of your own life.

2. Compare that safety to places and people that controlled your life in the past and are controlling it now.

Making Sense of What Makes No Sense

In his book, The Accidental Mind, neuroscientist Dr. David Linden tells us that our creative brain can take the raw material of the memory of a situation and weave it into a consistent yet bizarre story.[43] Thus, each person at a crime scene or accident can have a different account as to what happened.

Depending on how your stress system is activated, the neocortex will use what you see and the "facts" to create a story incorporating all the factors to have a smooth flow. But it often works through the lens of emotions. A person caught in a fear response will see fearful circumstances and justify their response even when the answer is bizarre.[44]

Memory is distributed in the brain, not reduced to any one region. Different types of memory are contained in different groups of areas. Many structures are involved in remembering because they include sights, smells, sounds, and many other sensations.[45] There are probably 10 to 30 different brain regions involved. Our brain links memories together that have a common thread, which helps in survival, future planning, and creativity but can cause faulty or false memories and loss of some detail of the individual memories.[46]

Drs. Garry and Wade provided 20 subjects with a picture of when the subjects were young in a hot air balloon ride with their family member. They had three interviews space 3-7 days apart, checking to see if they remembered the ride. At first, none remembered it. By the third interview, 50% of the people remembered complete or partial memories of the ride. It, however, never happened. The pictures of the subjects in the balloon were photoshopped. [47] Even more astounding, then others in another part of the experiment were given a narrative about their ride as opposed to a picture, 82% remembered the false memory. [48]

Psychologist Elizabeth Loftus, in a famous experiment, convinced a quarter of her participants they were once lost in a shopping center as a child, even when their family said it wasn't true. [49]

Professor of Psychology Christopher French of the University of London tells us that memory does not work like a video camera, recording every detail of an experience. When we recall an event, we reconstruct it based upon some more or less accurate memory bits. However, the brain will often automatically fill in any gaps without us being aware of it. "We remember the gist but not the details." Traumatic experience suffered later in life may be distorted and incomplete. [50]

In the book, The Science of False Memory- Oxford University Press, research has shown through many studies that we can even create false memories that never happened. [51]

The implications of this in forgiving are critical. From what you saw and the "facts" you have, the story you tell yourself might not be accurate. It may easily be a story created by your brain to smooth out the event for you to look good and be right.

We like to think we see, think, and remember clearly, but in truth, often we don't. There are gaps in our memory and thinking. We have a brain not built on reasoning but reaction. It tries to make sense of senseless situations by adding to them. [52] This must be considered when forgiving yourself and others!

To help look more reasonably at a person you have an upset with, try this.

1. Take a small upset you recently had with someone. Can you see how your side of the argument could change after talking it out and finding out what the other person was going through?

2. Since you are not always right, even when you think you are, can you see how this might be critical in your forgiveness work?

These are processes in the brain that are self-protective, tricking us into thinking we are right and that others are wrong. These reasons cause people to remain miserable. In the next chapters, I address all the blocks that keep us reluctant to forgive.

Chapter 8
How to Keep Stressed-Brain Reactions from Overriding Your Thinking and Creativity

Conflict and Stress

There are always at least two sides to a conflict. Conflict, by its definition, is stressful. When we judge and attack people based on our own opinion of what is right, we risk being wrong, even when we "know" we are right. In the search for truth, we must look more deeply at stress reactions and their effects. Some of the significant parts of forgiving in this chapter are coping with stress, emotional pain, effectively controlling stressed brain takeovers, and permanently forgiving.

Because unforgiven situations create stress for us, we need to look more deeply at how to alleviate our reactions to stress to forgive easily and be happy. This chapter deals with tensions, which might be from family, life, or trauma, and its sometimes-serious consequences.

Please Note: Behavior patterns are hard to change because they are often connected to early pleasure and safety experiences. To successfully change them, you need to ensure that pleasure and safety are in the new pattern.[1]

If you get angry with yourself when trying to employ new practices, you defeat their purpose by adding in stress rather than pleasure.

You will not control all the stress responses in your body and mind, but with knowledge, practice, and forgiveness, these reactions have less power over you.

When you become overstressed, and your functioning is significantly dimmed. These symptoms can show up:

- Distraction and hyperactivity
- Lack of determination.
- Impulse control issues.

- Chronic lateness and other time management issues, and
- Disorganization and procrastination.[2]

Journal Exercise
1. Do you see any connection between your stress and the above responses to it?

2. Look at your unforgiven situation. Can you step out of being a victim of it and move into an observer role so that you are watching yourself? Write down what you find.

3. From an observer's perspective, what might be in your past that makes you react the way you do to this situation?

4. Consider why you have these reactions? Journal your answers.

Protection in Stressful Situations

Stress, setbacks, and even trauma are part of life. How we deal with them up to us. Some people manage stress well; others do not. But this is not an accident. People who do well in the face of adversity have gained the ability to cope with crisis. This is called "resilience."

Resilience

Resilience is the ability to thrive, adapt, and cope despite challenging and stressful times.[3] It is forged by learning from mistakes enabling the person to cope with future undesirable situations. Studies show that helping people bounce back from adversities by acquiring self-regulation skills such as goal-setting and adjusting their path after a misstep equips them to do well in life.[4]

You can build your resilience by:
- Knowing your strengths and keeping them in mind.

- Building your self-esteem — have confidence in your abilities and the positive things in life.
- Building healthy relationships.
- Knowing when to ask for help.
- Managing stress and anxiety levels and
- Working on problem-solving skills and coping strategies. [4a]

"It's not something you're born with. It's something that gets built over time."-Dr. Jack Shonkoff, MD, Harvard University.[5]

Journal Exercise

- Can you think of a time when you exhibited resilience in the face of a really tough situation?

- What gives you hope and strength during hard times?

- What strategies or methods help you build resilience when facing adversity in your everyday life?

Good news! When researchers studied adolescents who had Adverse Childhood Experiences when they were 11 years old or younger, the ones who were doing well had developed a vital brain circuit for regulating emotion, which aids in resilience.[6] You can do the same thing with practicing forgiveness.

Resilience also helps repair the structural brain problems resulting from the trauma or adversity, allowing a person to recover.[7]

Dr. Ellen Walser deLara, a family therapist and professor of social work, interviewed more than 800 people age 18 to 65 who had been intensely bullied as children. Interestingly, about 47 percent of those interviewed said they had gotten something beneficial, like a sense of inner strength or self-reliance or empathy due to the experience.[8]

This is an excellent example of people gaining resilience from experiencing trauma. Research points us to two good ways to decrease the effects of trauma. These are developing empathy and an inner sense of strength.[9]

Breaking Out of Negative Thought Cycles

When bad things happen, we can get stuck repeatedly thinking about those incidents, what we could have done differently, or how we might mess up again in the future. We mistakenly believe that thinking about our misfortunes and difficulties will help us solve them. Unfortunately, this doesn't work and often keeps us from taking the actions to move forward.[10]

Here are more specific resilience-building skills that can be learned:

Stressed Thinking That Sabotages Forgiving

I've found three main ways that we sabotage our thinking and happiness:[11] Here they are with some exercise you can do.

1. Focusing on the Negative and Rejecting the Positive

Journal Exercise

a. In a problem area of your life, look for all the positives you can find. As much as possible, try saying, "What is positive in this?" and "What have I gained from this?"

b. Do this even when you think you can't.

c. Try to forgive the negatives in that person/event directly, remembering that the other person might be doing the very best she or he can do.

2. Black-and-White Thinking

In this reactive thinking, there is only good or bad. There are no in-between shades of color. Note that there is no gray. Parts of our brain think this way – they see only safety or danger. They only see opposites. Yet, life is multifaceted, as are people.

Remember: When we forgive other's imperfections, we exercise the muscle of forgiving ourselves.

Journal Exercise

a.   List all of the behaviors or qualities for which you have condemned yourself now and in the past.

b.   Look at your answers realistically and assign approximate percentages to each entry regarding how often you do that behavior or show that quality.[12]

c.   Then forgive yourself for each one.

3. Catastrophe Thinking (Catastrophizing)

This way of thinking sees disaster in every undesirable event encountered. To step out of an immediate catastrophe response, one needs to quiet the stress-reacting system. Take a walk, call a friend, do the Relaxation Response, etc.

Once you are calmed down, do the exercise below.

Journal on the Three Negative Thinking Styles

1.   Review these types of thinking – Focusing on the Negative and Rejecting the Positive, Black-and-White Thinking, and Catastrophe Thinking – Journal what is similar about them.

2. Observe what is happening in each one from an objective perspective – detached from your reactions. Write about what you find.

3. For catastrophizing, do the following: [13]

    a. Make a list of what you think will occur because of what happened.

    b. With each item, ask, "Is it true?"

    c. Then ask, "How do I know it will happen?"

    d. Look for positive possibilities that could occur for each

    e. Note any behaviors or qualities for which you condemn others or yourself.

    f. See if you can forgive yourself or the others for each item.

    g. Save this list, as you will use it again soon.

If you can't do these right now, carry on reading the chapters and doing the exercises provided. Catastrophe/disaster thinking takes more than forgiveness to resolve. Though forgiving helps to deal with parts of the catastrophe, dealing with this type of thinking also takes trust and faith in Life and connecting with the most authentic part of us, which is beyond this book's scope. That journey of connecting with the core and most authentic part of us, I feel, is our main one. For me, that core is Love, peace, and joy. Forgiveness helps a lot to clear the way.

Negative thought cycles can become well-worn pathways in our brains. To change them, we need to short-circuit our thoughts. Try exercising, taking a walk, or doing a breathing exercise for a few minutes to calm down our anxiety.[14]

Overcoming Fear of Failure

Really, the fourth stressed thinking that sabotages forgiving is fear of failure. Failure is deeply human. Everyone, no matter their background, skill, or life story, each person will fail spectacularly at least once in their life and often much more in my experience. The problem with failure is perspective. Often when we look back at our failures it is from the perspective of who we are now as opposed to hwo we were then and the resources available at that time. My mistakes/failures at 22-year-old were the result of knowledge and perspectives I had then. I judged myself for years because of those mistakes, which was fool hardy and caused much unneeded regret. When I reassessed what I knew then I understood my decisions in that light, which made all the difference.

Learning to be okay with making mistakes, big or small, is an essential skill—one tied to resilience and future success (and undoubtedly forgiving of self and others). One recent study found that young scientists who experienced a significant setback early in their career went on to greater success than scientists who had seen early wins.[15]

Journal exercise

Look at each of your failures in life. Spend time with each and answer these questions:

1. Did I do the best I could at the time with the knowledge and resources I had?

2. What was positive from the experience that helped me later in life?

3. What was negative that I learned from it and have not forgiven?

4. What of each can you forgive?

Other Strategies for Becoming More Resilient

Getting enough sleep, eating well, and exercising can reduce stress, which may, in turn, boost resilience. But also nurturing close relationships can help.

Regularly thinking about morals and actively living according to one's values have been linked to higher resilience.[16] Dr. Ellen Hendriksen, a clinical psychologist at Boston University's Center for Anxiety and Related Disorders, tells us, "If you don't know what to do, look to your values. A handful of studies have found that having a moral compass—an internal system of values and ethics—goes along with higher resilience. Strong ethics and morality seem to give purpose to our lives, which in turn gives rise to resilience."[17]

Any crisis, such as the 2019-21 coronavirus pandemic, tests our resilience. What helps you weather almost any storm are:

- looking to loved ones for help and emotional support,
- increasing self-care, and
- focusing on what you can control in a situation.[18]

Calming Exercises Using the Breath

Breathing awareness methods are used in every part of the world. You'd be surprised how taking control of the breath changes the stress reaction.

Most people breathe from the top of their chests. This causes stress in the body because the person does not take in enough oxygen that way. The ideal way to breathe is to get the breath to the bottom of the lungs. The belly should expand when breathing in and contract when breathing out.

You can put your hand on your belly to be aware of your hand's rise and fall when breathing. This skill alone can be helpful to take your mind off an upset.

Once you can do this easily, a breathing method I like for stress reduction is called "Square Breathing." It works for old and young. If you have a child, have them imagine a square in front of them and start where they want to outline their breathing with their finger:

a. Breathe in for four counts as you trace the first side of the square.
b. Hold your breath for four counts as you trace the second side of the square

c. Breathe out for four counts as you trace the third side of the square
d. Hold your breath for four counts as you trace the final side of the square
e. That completed one deep breath! And start again.[19]

Do this for at least five cycles, depending on how much this calms you.

Additional Effective Stress Reduction Methods To Use

Laughter is excellent medicine. It reduces stress hormones in the body and increases the release of endorphins—the body's natural feel-good hormones.

Squeezing something is an effective way to release tension. You can use squeeze balls to calm down and manage stress.[20]

Music that is calming and soothing is another powerful way to handle stress. The sounds of water, rain, waves, wind, birds singing also have a calming effect.[21]

The healing power of water is quite effective in lowering your anxiety. You can take a refreshing shower or a nice hot bath. If you are stressing out, remember to make sure you have plenty of water to drink.[22]

Cuddling and connecting emotionally decreases stress hormones. Holding someone's hand or hugging or cuddling with a pet are all useful and restore a feeling of inner peace and calm.[23]

- How can you increase each one of the above in your life?

Notes

Chapter 9
What Makes Forgiving Difficult

The Deadly Rules, Judgments, and Expectations

As we've talked of previously, much of the difficulty we have in forgiving comes from the emotional and survival norms learned by us as children through our family, culture, religion, and society in which we live. Research tells us that we need to be aware of our rules and norms that color the lens through which we view and judge people and their actions if we want to forgive or care to reconcile with someone or group, especially if our rules influence us not to trust the other.[1]

Also, establishing and rebuilding trust and respect are an integral part of developing love in a family and intimate relationships. However, our rules can color our expectations of others' behavior, influencing a negative view and trust of them.

No matter the age, we operate using a set of rules and codes of behavior. We need to identify those that might not be valid and might even be destructive to ourselves in self-forgiveness and harm a relationship we are in or desire.

A child who experiences domestic violence might try that behavior to influence other children who do not obey their wishes. A child who bullies learned that behavior from somewhere—often a parent or sibling. One study found that fathers who were bullies when they were in school were more likely to have children who bully.[2]

Journal exercise

To evaluate the validity and validity of your values, laws, rules, or moral codes, you can do this:

1. List the values, laws, rules, or moral codes that you feel your offender has broken.

2. Looking at each, ask:

    a. Where did this rule come from?

    b. At present, is it a beneficial rule or code? Or is it one that needs revision?

3. Then ask: Do I have an unrealistic expectation of another to follow that law, value, or rule, particularly if I have failed to follow it in some way relative to others or myself?

4. Do I have an unrealistic expectation for myself to obey that law, value, or rule?

5. Can I forgive the other and myself once I see the rules I have?

The Desire for Justice, Retaliation, and Revenge

In his book, *Beyond Revenge: The Evolution of the Forgiveness Instinct*, prominent forgiveness researcher, Dr. Michael McCullough, describes using magnetic resonance imaging (MRI) to observe the brains of people who wanted revenge and retaliation against someone who had harmed them. His work showed that the brain is hard-wired for justice.

As hunter-gatherers, we needed a mechanism in place to keep peace in a tribe. Making amends became essential for the group to remain together and function well. McCullough and other researchers show why we often feel that we need at least an apology or some kind of compensation to demonstrate a sincere intention to make things right after a harmful mistake. By making amends, we or another feel satisfied to reconcile and work together again in the tribe.[3]

The researchers call this "the injustice gap." "When people harm others or break social rules, there is a gap between the way that things are and how they would be if things were fair." We can reduce the gap and restore justice through apologies, attempts at communication and understanding, or even via the offender's punishment.[4]

In the book *Natural Conflict Resolution*, Filippo Aureli and Frans de Waal document reconciliation in 27 species of primates, as well as goats and other mammals. Other research with dolphins shows similar reconciliation moves.[5]

With humans, the problem can be that each of the parties in conflict often sees the situation differently and often blames the other. Witnesses have their observations taken into account by those who run a justice system of some sort to determine if their observations are valid.

When we are part of a very large population, there is less possibility of reencountering the other party to resolve the injustice gap. For example, consider your chances of restitution in a metropolitan area hit-and-run accident. McCullough proposes that forgiveness becomes the mechanism that can change your upset because the other option is to remain angry and in pain over what happened.[6] Since forgiveness comes from the highest functions of the prefrontal lobes of the neocortex.[7] It evolved to restrain our reaction to be vengeful, alleviating the stress that revenge puts on us.[8]

Justice Systems and The Brain

Justice systems are built on making amends. Break the law, and you have to compensate a person, group, or society somehow, like going to jail or paying a fine.

The part of the brain most engaged in the desire for justice and revenge turns out to be the same region that gets excited by fulfilling a craving. That's right, retaliation and revenge initially stimulate the reward pathways of the brain.[9] Even so, studies also have shown that when vengeance is taken, the person, in general, is not happier because he or she continues to obsess over what happened and thus stays stressed.[10, 11]

The desire to punish, often through revenge or justice, was a useful emotion when humans lived in smaller societies. In those times, the consequences of revenge/justice would have effectively deterred anti-social behavior because working together was the only way for the community to survive.[12] But in modern times, relying on fear of retaliation or compensation delivered through the justice system might not obtain the results we want, as the judge might make a finding against you and in favor of your offender.

The examples of our desire for justice and revenge plus research showing we are wired to absorb negativity and enjoy revenge[13] make it clear that our brains are the largest barrier to forgiving. It's no wonder forgiveness is such a difficult task.

However, if we apply our brain to a few tried-and-true forgiveness techniques, they can become a daily part of who we are, what we stand for, and what we do each day. Those actions can become the foundation for world peace.

Journal question

- How do you see your desire for justice in the situation(s) you are dealing with?

- Will you get the justice you want, considering the effect it might be having on your body and mind?

Concern for Fairness as a Barrier to Forgiving

The thought that another is mistreating you can interfere with your forgiveness attempts and actions. What's fair is often tough to agree on because your "offender" sees things differently. This unfair perspective is the desire for justice built into the brain. But it doesn't help forgiving.[14]

Journal Exercise

1. Write down a time when you felt one way about an upset, and the other person felt differently.

2. What were the two feelings expressed?

3. Was yours correct? Did it make your life better? Or were you being stubborn and focused on being "right"?

4. How is this kind of "being right" helpful to you?

5. Write down how this exercise has expanded your ability to forgive another.

How Our Outer World Reflects Our Inner One

The world we see is often upsetting. But in reality, what we see are just particles or waves of light in patterns. Light comes through the eye to the optical nerve to the brain. The brain then interprets those patterns before we know what we are seeing. To do this, the brain must access its experience and information data stockpile, which interprets what it sees and the emotions tied to it.

In our first years, we rapidly fill our information stockpile. We learn to identify our surroundings initially from the first people in our lives. They teach us what things are and do, and naturally pass on their emotional biases about those items. Because we build our information network together with similar items, we interpret all our other experiences through our first teachers—Mom, Dad, siblings, and others close to us, and our experiences with them. Our mother is our primary emotional and information source; her information is even transmitted through the womb.[15] Therefore, your initial teachers greatly influence how you see and feel the world.

Even something as simple as color may create a strong emotional reaction. If a mother hates red because of a trauma she experienced, she may pass that bias along to her child. The child does not have to be told red is bad. The child will pick it up in voice inflection and facial expression of the mother, influencing the child.[16]

A child raised in an abusive household will often see the world as unsafe, to be feared. Similarly, a child raised by a paranoid parent often will be fearful of people and surroundings.[17] Because of the fear that the parent and child have, their stressed brain reactions are more active. Hence, there is less opportunity for rational thinking and positive emotions. As a result, fear will be more constant, and the family will experience less joy.

Conversely, a child raised with love feels safer and sees the world as a safer place than one who is beaten or abused in some other way. The child who feels safe will be happier and think more clearly because their neocortex will be functioning more due to flight and fight not being active. Many studies have shown that children raised without human touch in their first year of life tend to die, and if they survive, they have poor emotional responses to people and life.[18]

As you see, what is going on inside of us determines how we see the world. The stressed-brain reactions are influenced primarily by our familial, cultural, and religious teachings and bias.

Oddly, we still accept and use our early programming from persons we do not now respect or agree with. Therefore, to change a habitual reaction, you have to look at your original indoctrination and make a strong effort to transform it. This is not easy because our early training and emotional reactions have been a part of us for many years and often come from the earliest brains' reactions.

Nevertheless, the freedom gained by examining our behavioral rules and expectations of others is invaluable. Psychotherapy can help in this examination.

At age 55, Allen was discouraged about ever finding a partner. He was a professional, good-looking, and smart, yet he had never been in a long-term relationship. In one of my university forgiveness classes, he expressed that he had a hard time forgiving his mother for being so restricting. Thus, he decided to look deeply at all his initial training from his mother—he called it "brainwashing." He especially searched for her subtle messages and rules.

"This was the toughest thing I've done in my life," Allen admitted. "I hated the way my mother treated me as a kid. She was too protective and too concerned about everything I did. She was hurt when I didn't give her enough attention. What surprised me when I looked at our relationship is that I expected other women to give me extraordinary attention. When they didn't, it was obvious they didn't like me." He added, "No wonder I have never been in a long-term relationship. I never gave anyone a chance. The truth is, I didn't want ever to be smothered again, and even worse, I felt I could never do enough for any partner. I saw women as bottomless pits. That was unfair to every woman I went out with." He understood why his mother was that way and forgave her.

This shows us how Allen's outer world reflected his inner world. Allen's ability to see how his early programming ran his life was profound. Because our paths crossed socially, I was aware that he did develop a loving relationship within a year of taking the class.

A person who is taught early on that another race is bad and evil will likely see those people negatively until there is a different set of messages put into the brain. We are given many prejudices and negative responses in our early life. These continue to affect us even as adults because we can only interpret what is going on for us using the information we already have. Forgiveness enables us to change our habitual responses.

Here is another example of how our inner experience affects our outer one. Possibly, you had experienced driving through a town when you were hungry. Maybe the lack of restaurants influenced what you think of the town. If you are angry, you might only see unfriendly people and problems. Another person in the car might be affected by something else and react differently to the town. When asked about the town, each person in the car will have a different response, some even strongly emotional.

Your Thoughts, Your Choice, Your Healing

Healing results from a simple principle of the mind: Your thoughts cannot go in opposing directions simultaneously and get anywhere. For example, you can't hate and love very well at the same time. People say you can love the person and hate what they did. I question that because hate activates the fight/flight system where love has no entry. You can disagree and love, but not hate and love too well. Hold onto upsets and remain in the dark. Let go and lighten up.

To me, therefore, the question in forgiveness work becomes: "Where are you putting your mind, and do you want to keep it there? Is it on the positive where you feel good or the negative where you feel bad?" That could be a practical question for you.

Here are several forgiveness methods to assist.

a. If you want peace, focus your mind on peace and send it to your offender or offenders from your heart.

b. Say prayers to them and yourself. You can especially use the Lovingkindness Blessing.

c. Fill your mind with love as best as you can. Then send that love to the offender as well as yourself.

d. Journal how you feel doing each.

These are only a few ways to clear the upset and have a happier outlook. Your challenge is to feed yourself what you need. If chaos reigns, choose peace.

Journal Exercise – Being Positive

1. Can you maintain a loving attitude and pleasant thoughts at the same time as being angry, feeling rage, being bitter, or having a desire for revenge?

2. If not, what would help, do you think?

3. Explain how holding a loving attitude brings back your ability to be positive and at peace.

Inner Strength

When I was in my early twenties after college, I worked on a small private cruise ship. The staff and crew had a lot of stress due to overly punitive officers. To get away from it all one day, I went to the forward part of the ship to see out over the dark blue sea and bright blue sky to the white clouds on the horizon. From my early religious experiences, I knew I was much more than my current negative emotional state. In my confusion and sadness, I realized that I was not the victim of what was going on. Then I experienced a profound inner state of strength. It was calm, empowering, and not fearful or angry. Through the years, I have used that sense of inner strength when I need to.

- Do you remember a time when you felt a calm inner strength? Perhaps it was in sports or accomplishing something else you worked for where you felt empowered or peaceful. Write about it and see if you can access that feeling.

- Practice accessing it throughout the day.

A Sense of Truth

Our inner sense of the truth is our conscience. We shut it down when we argue, justify, insist we are right, or don't listen to others. In that "shut-down" state, we might attack others who disagree with us. Our upsets are consequences of how our heavy protective armor prevents compassion, love, and healing.

Acknowledging our inner sense of truth, our conscience, always puts us on the right path to forgiving. How do we know it's right? There is a sense of rightness within that is calming and empowering. It does not desire attack because the fight-and-flight part of the brain is not engaged. In this state, we are not angry or fearful. It's the inner state of strength I mention in a previous section.

1. In that state, can you consider that you may not know the whole truth about a hurtful situation?

2. Might that calm state help you to let go of the situation? If so, how?

3. If you were willing to put aside your justifications about being right, how would it help you forgive someone?

4. If you were willing to listen to your conscience, your inner sense of what is right, how would that help your forgiveness work?

The Forgiveness Battle

The battle between resentment and forgiveness is the split between <u>our basic survival self</u> vs. <u>our authentic and true self.</u>

- Our highest, authentic, and true self gives us clear thinking, our loftiest vision for life, and goals of community, peace, and kindness.

- Our fundamental "survival self" protects us by alerting us to dangers and setting limits on others. In doing so, it keeps us small, depressed, fearful, vengeful, and very self-centered when it's in constant control. That is the result of maintaining the armor for too long.

Both "selves" are needed, but to overcome the basic, survival self-centeredness, you need to understand its mechanisms so that your highest or authentic self-- the part that enjoys life, thinks clearly, loves others, and is peaceful—can prevail in your life. It's a constant struggle!! Forgiveness helps tremendously.

Being aware of the forgiveness battle helps you develop your sense of your highest/authentic self and identify primarily with that more than just focusing on survival.

Deciding to Forgive

As you apply these forgiveness techniques, you may encounter an incident that you can't resolve no matter what you try. One simple action you can do is to decide to forgive the person(s) involved anyway. This is where you remove the heavy armor of resentment and put it to the side, accessing your inner strength. It takes effort but is worth it. The more you do it, the easier it becomes.

Journal Exercise

Look at a situation that troubles you and ask:

1. What is the highest goal you have for doing this work?

2. Are you willing to work on this challenging situation?

3. What is the benefit of forgiving this person?

4. Are you committed to freeing yourself from the negative consequences in your life that this situation is causing you?

5. What is preventing you from deciding to let it go now?

6. (If something is preventing it) What can you do to resolve this block?

Deciding to forgive is an ability you develop. The more you decide and feel the actual change inside, the better you become at it. The "I forgive" exercise in an earlier chapter does not necessarily bring about a decision to forgive but just a movement in the heart where forgiveness occurs. A decision might come from that "I forgive" process, but not always.

Developing the Power of Decision

Deciding to forgive is an essential step in making forgiving easier. The decision to forgive can be powerful and comes more easily by understanding what your offender has gone through in their life – for example, walking in their shoes. As you keep reading and doing the exercises, you gain enough knowledge of unforgiven situations and enough compassion for those involved, including yourself, to make it easier to decide to let upsets go.

1. Compared to when you began this workbook, how do you feel about deciding to forgive someone now? Please write it down.

2. What do you need to do to incorporate this decision into your daily life? Write it down.

Our Perfection Standards

Often, we hold others and ourselves to unrealistic standards due to our unrealistic expectations of perfection. Identifying our standards and re-evaluating them is central to forgiving and to being content.

Though we like to think that critical analysis helps us function better, we often misuse it to judge and condemn. Thus, we keep others and ourselves in the debris of failure instead of empowering us to get up, brush off, and move on.

Standards, values, and rules for living are necessary to the fabric of our social, religious, personal development, expression, and expansion. The problem comes when our judgments lead us to condemn and attack others or ourselves.

Attacking others in our mind or in life brings unhappiness at the least and tragedy at the extreme. Just look at the decimation of peoples and cultures in Rwanda and Bosnia in recent times and the ongoing threats of jihad and terrorism.

I am not advocating lowering standards, but instead, identifying where your values come from and determining if they are truly appropriate. I am promoting being less judgmental toward yourself and others when they don't meet "your" standards. If you deem that the standards are valuable, keep using them. But sometimes, they can be harmful. For instance, Ben's father had been an athlete. He coached his son well and had him in good shape early in his life. Ben proceeded to excel in sports as he had high standards, and he was very fit. But he made fun of weaker, less-skilled kids, mocking them and being a bully.

1. How do you judge others who are not as good or skilled as you are?

2. How can compassion, forgiveness, and "walking in the other's shoes" help.

Writing Dialogue

A useful tool in forgiving is writing about your experience concerning a specific situation concerning yourself, another, or others. I call this the Dialogue Process. I've used this writing technique for years to get underneath the upset to see it in a new light. This shift in viewpoint is critical in the whole effort of letting go.

The questions and answers never fail to surprise. Try starting with an inner request for guidance and help, if you are spiritual, a prayer. I've found that help often comes.

Journal Exercise

Here is what you can say:

1. Start by conversing with yourself about your upset. Write down the first question (Q1) you want an answer to.

2. Write down what comes to your mind.

3. You'll find that your next question will then come up. Be curious.

4. Always continue on the next logical question.
   a. For example, if you are upset with your brother or sister, write what happened and the extent of your upset. Wait for a question to come up, perhaps, "How could he do that?" Answer the question and write it down. Ask the next question that comes up. And so on.

5. When emotions come up, accept them, keep writing, or ask another question, like "What's behind this emotion?"

6. Keep doing this until you get a new understanding of the situation, or you feel a wave of compassion or relief come up.

Wellness

People who harm others intentionally are not well in some way. It could be physical, mental, spiritual, or emotional pain that could be causing their actions. Individuals are a complex mixture of reactions. You don't know their upbringing, the violence, abuse, or trauma they have had in their lives that could affect their present behavior. That doesn't mean you must involve the offender in your life, but it should not prevent you from forgiving them.

I found it very difficult to forgive my father because of his abusiveness over the years. It was not until I remembered that he was in continual pain from injuries in WWII that my upset disappeared. Forgiveness happened with that "aha! moment." It took no effort. However, it took years to reach that realization.

Notes

Chapter 10
Practices That Enhance Power of The Heart, Compassion, And Love for Forgiving

In this chapter, we go into the power of the heart, compassion, love, and practices to enhance them for forgiving. These are from my own experience, without going into religion. If my perspective helps, fine. It might give you a view to work with if you seek a different way of looking at the chaos around life and religions today.

A Higher Power in Forgiving

Through the years, I've found that people's concept of a Higher Power, God, Allah, or whatever term they prefer, both positively and negatively influences their forgiving. Having a positive perspective of a helping and loving Divinity can make them more accepting of forgiveness.

On the other hand, some people see this "divine aspect" primarily as a judge and condemner, which justifies their condemning and harming others. They also use the same justification to blame themselves, which explains their suffering and pain. Some people feel that God, or whatever term used, is unjust, causes tragedies, makes terrible decisions, takes sides, and does not help when asked, or is not the God they thought He was. This questioning is common when people consider forgiving tragedies or face their own deep crises. By forgiving God, you can support your forgiveness in these circumstances. Break down all the things you feel God did that weren't right. See if you can forgive each issue.

Theological questioning is beyond this book's scope and is for your religious leader to help you. I had many upsets with "God," which caused me to re-evaluate and figure out who or what God was for me practically and theologically. In my forgiveness work concerning "God," I realized that humans, including myself, had caused all the upsets I experienced.

The Magnitude of the Creative Force

There are said to be 100 billion galaxies in the universe. To get an idea of the size of a billion, if you tapped your finger every second continually and each day only took off 8 hours for sleeping and eating, after about 70 years, you would tap out a billion. Our galaxy, The Milky Way, is a medium-sized galaxy with 200 billion stars. Our average-sized Sun is only one of those stars. I cannot conceive of the magnitude of our universe's size, nor can I possibly consider understanding what the Creative Force is that brought it all about. Each religion calls that help something different. You can call that Force whatever you want.

I no longer blame things on "God" when I can't conceive that magnitude of existence. I simply know I have intuitive help. But again, I am reticent to put a name onto it. In this book, I attempt to name the quality without its many religious terms. I prefer the term "intuition."

Cleaning up the heart and mind of all resentments and even judgments, an ongoing experience of love, peace, and joy is available to all of us. I want everyone to have this experience, which is why I have been teaching and counseling for over 27 years.

The Core of Our Being - The Heart - The Altar of Love and Joy

When we look, we see compassionate, forgiving people surrounding us. They give care and even give their lives for strangers. What is that? Why is that? It is the principle of Love, which to me is The Principle of Life. Without It, self-centeredness would destroy everything for its own sake, blind to its self-sabotage.

When one chooses Love as his or her guiding principle, then judgments are only ideas against Love. Those judgments might be culturally or politically correct, but, in my experience, they can interfere with the loving perspective and experience. It's paradoxical—the judgment is accurate, but its consequences can be detrimental to us.

Earlier in this workbook, I mentioned that I experience love and compassion at the core of my being. Through my love or heartfulness experience, I connect with a part of myself that is united to people, nature, and Life itself. It is more real than that part of me that runs around going places and doing things. It's a calm place, and I feel fulfilled just being in it, which is why I practice meditation. When I meditated before my forgiveness transformation, I would eventually experience a very content feeling by the end of the meditation. After my forgiveness transformation, that contentment I had worked to reach is where I would start my meditations.

Hint: I often set a timer to go off regularly during the day to remind me not to go so far away from what I consider my "real" self.

Love and Forgiveness

Letting go of negative emotions, feelings, and guilt brings us back to re-experiencing love, peace, and joy. Without love as the foundation in our lives and hearts, I've seen we succumb more easily to loss and lack, making life unpleasant and often unbearable. This was an undeniable experience in my life.

- How does doing an unloving act, such as belittling someone even though you feel they might deserve it, really make you feel?

The Lovingkindness Affirmation

Affirming or blessing others is a great way to get to forgiving yourself and others. And an excellent way to do self-nurturing. Do the lovingkindness blessing that I addressed in Chapter 3. You will get the benefit. It might or might not help others, but it will help the person saying it. There are many variations—some call it a prayer, and some use it as a meditation, even for 5-day extended retreats.

> May you be safe.
> May you be well.
> May you be happy.
> May you be free from suffering.
> May you be filled with love and kindness.
> May you be filled with joy.
> May you be at peace and at ease.

Here is a breakdown of the different aspects of it and the recommendation for using them.

Safety – We addressed this in Chapter 2,

Question: When you read, "May you be safe!" How does it feel, and what do you think of it?

Wellness- We addressed this in the last chapter.
  Ask
  1. How do you feel when you read, "May you be well"?

  2. Is the person you are trying to forgive unwell in some way that might be causing what they did?

Happiness – Being happy takes many things in life going well, especially inside one's mind. Rich people commit suicide. Successful people commit suicide. Years ago, as a volunteer Law Enforcement Chaplain, I went on a suicide call to a noted professional's home. He seemed to have everything going for him--success, money, status, and loving family-- yet he ended his life. It seemed that I was doing well in 1993. I had good friends, some status, teaching at a university, a psychotherapist, and I still came close to ending my own life. It's difficult to know what is going on with others.

  Exercise
  1. How do you feel when you read: "May you be happy"?

  2. If the offender was happy with their life and with him or herself, would they have done what they did to you?

  3. Wishing someone to be well doesn't hurt us and indeed might be good for us.

Freedom from Suffering – We all suffer in some way. A person who intentionally harms another is suffering, or they would not want others to have pain. A suffering person is certainly not happy, probably not feeling safe, not well either physically, emotionally, mentally, or spiritually. Compassion for people who have harmed us because they hurt inside brings us more peace than wanting them to suffer. Your own pain and suffering actually increase when you desire suffering for another person,[1] because you are focusing your mind on suffering, rather than the peace, joy, or love that would make them feel better.

1. How do you feel when you read, "May you be free from suffering"?

2. What would it be like to walk in the shoes of the person you are upset with?

Lovingkindness – This is a quality different than kindness and just being loving. As an example, I was regularly serving food at a homeless center. Having been a building contractor early on in my life, I am production-minded, looking at the best use of time to do what is being done. One woman was slowing things down! She took the time and interest to ask each adult and each child what they would like. I knew I was being nice enough and kind, but I had an assembly-line attitude. She showed sweetness and caring to each person who came by her. I was serving and getting the job done; she was serving and blessing each person. That, to me, is what lovingkindness is—an extra effort in kindness and love.

1. When you read, "May you be filled with Lovingkindness!" what do you feel?

2. Who do you know would benefit from that level of kindness and love? If so, can you send it to them?

3. Where would you like more lovingkindness in your own life?

Joy – It is hard for me to describe the difference between love and joy. Sure, I know when I feel love for someone, it is different than joy. But at a spiritual level, since I have had love as a pretty constant awareness in my heart through the day, it also feels joyful. That's not to say I've got it together. I am a terror when I drive, but I can catch myself, laugh off my stupidity and foolishness, and return to joy. Sometimes it takes a deep meditation to sort myself out.

Joy is not necessarily happiness. It is not there because of accomplishing anything or getting something. It is a feeling of contentment that doesn't rely on good fortune/outside conditions. Life lacks richness when joy is not there. When I don't feel joy, I find where I have judged or resented. The moment I spot my upset and let it go, joy returns almost magically. A few times, when I've had a resentment that I could not forgive, Joy was gone for months until I found a way to let the upset go. I've been doing this "clean up" for 27 years.

1. How do you feel when you read, "May you be filled with Joy!"?

2. How would your life change if you had Joy in it for no good reason?

3. Would that be the inspiration for holding no resentment or judgment toward others or yourself?

4. What would that take?

Inner Peace – Our inner peace depends on our state of mind--a lack of fighting or running away, no fear, and no anxiety. Sure, experiences external to us can take away our sense of peace. Still, years of meditations have shown me that I can find inner peace again, even with an agitating external environment.

Our survival is dependent on being aware of our environment and trying to stay safe. I've taught meditation and stress management for years and have seen people find peace inside themselves even during frenetic activity and danger. For some, it is found by reading inspirational writings or scriptures, contemplating a figure or picture of a Divine Being, and for others, quieting the mind of its chatter and runaway thoughts.

Once, several emergency room nurses took my meditation course. I frequently teach and practice setting a timer for every hour to re-center for a couple of moments. That worked well for them. My students shared that by re-centering hourly, they rarely felt as stressed by the end of the day, because they were de-stressing every hour.

Ask:

1. When you read, "May you be at peace and at ease!" What comes to mind? How do you feel?

2. Who do you think could use this besides yourself?

Here is the blessing again in full:

May you be safe. May you be well. May you be happy. May you be free from suffering. May you be filled with love and kindness. May you be filled with joy. May you be at peace and at ease.

The shortened one is: May you be safe, well and happy; Free from suffering; and filled with Love, Joy and Peace.

Using Your Imagination

We have a tremendous capacity to use our imaginations. Relaxation and forgiveness are significant areas to work with to create an inner vision to improve a perspective about an experience. Hypnosis research is fascinating on the subject of changing our inner experience. A few years back, the New York Times reported, "What you see is not always what you get, because what you see depends on a framework built by experience that stands ready to interpret the raw information."[2] We have known this for a long time in hypnotherapy, but now science confirms it. When hypnotized people reviewed a past event and then changed it by picturing it differently, the brain acted as though the changed event was real. When the event was recalled later, as seen by MRI scans, the brain responded as if the new experience from hypnosis was real.[3]

Guided meditations also allow us to reinterpret and often change the experience of trauma. Research has shown that there are hypnosis methods that help relieve people of traumatic incidents. [4, 5, 6]

When you relax, breathe, and picture yourself, perhaps at a beach or in the mountains, and then make the picture and feelings seem real, the neural impulses will respond as if the situation actually occurred.[7] Doing this can transform your upsetting experience in minutes. It takes practice, but you will achieve the relaxation and mind shift you seek by working on it.

Here is a real example I know of showing the power of imagination. Maria was ready to quit her job when she came to see her hypnotherapist. "I hate my boss, and so does everyone else," she said in tears. Her boss had been unkind to her in front of other employees. She could not forgive him. With hypnosis, Maria pictured herself in her favorite beautiful nature scene and then had the boss enter that scene to apologize. Then the therapist asked her to picture hugging and forgiving her boss. She was not asked to forgive, but only to picture as if it had occurred. The session lasted 20 minutes. The next time her therapist saw her two weeks later, she was enthusiastic about her work and was getting along fine with the boss.

This is an example of the power of imagination in forgiving. You can use your creative imagination similarly anytime. The method has many popular names—creative visualization and self-hypnosis are the most common. It is a skill we all have; it only needs development and practice.

Using Your Imagination for Forgiving

Here is a Forgiveness Visualization that has been proven effective in getting the brain and mind into a more positive state. You might be surprised by what this activity can do. Often the brain focuses on negative scenarios very well. However, picturing a positive scenario is richer, more rewarding, and can bring more joy and peace in your life, especially for self-forgiveness.[8]

Here is a visualization that includes relaxation. First, find a quiet place where you can remain for fifteen to thirty minutes or longer without interruptions.

1. Close your eyes.

2. Relax any tensions you are aware of as much as you can. For just this exercise, let go of other concerns and focus on becoming calm.

3. Imagine love pouring into you in any way that you can, perhaps from a Divine Source or from anyone you can think of, real or imaginary, who can send you love. (This action, in itself, may be quite moving.)

4. When you feel love filling you, imagine the person who upsets you. Send love to that person. (You might even hug him or her in your mind.) Continue doing this until you feel something shift inside from a negative to a positive.

5. You'll notice that the more you give love, the more you feel it in return. You will not only feel better; you will also feel more forgiving.

6. Now see yourself taking the other person's point of view. See what he or she experiences and goes through in life.

7. Imagine forgiving the person. What would that feel like?

Meditation for Your Well-being and Heart

Through my years of teaching and practicing meditation, I've learned it is merely choosing where to put your awareness and keeping it there. It might be on a positive or neutral word, picture, statement, mental picture, or breathing. Every religion in the world uses it. You could just as easily use the term contemplation. Many people are overwhelmed by negative emotions from what's going on in their lives, school, work, and the news, and their minds focus on fear, hate, revenge, etc. People suffer the consequences of that negative focus – discontent, depression, rage, emotional disturbance, and unhappiness. Meditation focuses on the positive, being calmer and kinder in life, and it clears the mind of turmoil, disorder, and confusion.

Neuroscience research strongly indicates that meditation can make you think more clearly and be happier. Its other benefits are improved thinking, attention, response control, increased immune function, decreased stress, improved emotional control, and a slowdown of the effects of aging.[9, 10]

Success with any relaxation method or meditation comes from how well a person can relax so that the day's thoughts do not intrude so easily. I just gave several relaxation methods. These can be done at any time and are an excellent precursor to longer meditations. You can read them with the idea of becoming proficient at them in any way you find works. Eventually, you should be able to have the relaxation work using this simplified format naming the different parts of the major muscle groups.

For example:
1. Be aware of your head and tensions, aches, pains, stiffness, or soreness you might have in your forehead, back of the neck, and jaws. Let those discomforts go.

2. Focus on your shoulders, back, chest, arms, and hands, relaxing those areas.

3. And now focus on your belly, butt, and legs, relaxing those areas.

After you are experienced with the above, this should be enough:
♦ Starting with your head and working down, let all tensions, aches, pains, stiffness, or soreness drain out through your hands and feet.

From this relaxed state, we can go to the following powerful meditations.

Nurturing Your Heart

After you have done some sort of relaxation method, like the one above, do this:
1. Be aware of a sense of Love in your heart, perhaps for a family member or good friend. Increase it and feel that love extending out from you into the room.

2. Feel it naturally move out of your location and into your neighborhood.

3. Expand that love to fill your city. Have it fill the area surrounding your city, extending to loved ones, other people, the trees, countryside, and to other towns until Love touches your whole region.

4. Allow it to fill your nation, and then other nations, and even continents.

5. See and feel Love filling the earth, the ocean, and everything in it.

6. See the Love you are sending benefitting all life, including the person you are trying to forgive.

7. Sit with this for a few minutes appreciating what you are seeing and feeling.

8. Come back when you are ready.

9. Journal what happened.

Saying Positive Statements

You will see nice results using positive statements that you agree with as long as you include positive emotions to accompany those positive statements, and you say them often during the day.

My clients and students are always surprised by how many times a day they say negative things about themselves.

If you are experiencing constant negative emotions and upsets, do the following steps:

The first four steps will enable forgiving thoughts to take hold. All six will allow you to live the life you want to have.

Here is an example of negative comments caught and corrected: "That was stupid!" "No! I just didn't think it through but went on automatically. I think well when I apply myself." Forgiveness? "Sure, but I need to become more aware of what I am doing instead of daydreaming."

1. Carry your journal or a pad of paper throughout the day and note each time you say something negative about yourself. Write the statement down.

2. Make a positive emotional declaration to replace it. Write it down, then write or draw the result you want to see. This might take some creativity to come up with the correct statement.

3. When you can, forgive yourself for each negative statement as it comes up.

4. Go through your day doing this—forgiving and replacing every negative thought with a positive.

5. Continue writing both the negative and positive ones in your journal as you may want to see them from time to time.

6. Acknowledge yourself for catching the negative and forgiving yourself for each one. Acknowledge yourself for making a positive statement to replace the negative.

Notes

Chapter 11
Bullying and More Effective Tools for Forgiving

Sadly, almost one in three adults are bullied. The same statistic is for children, plus, many adults bullied as children still carry the scars. Forgiveness makes a difference. Because bullying has been found to have effects into adulthood, so I go into it so that a person who was bullied in childhood might find the information of value. There is hope. Plus, forgiveness can help much, obviously.

This chapter also contains additional techniques for finding deeper meaning in your forgiveness work and speeding it up.

Empathy, Compassion, and Sympathy

These show a connection and feelings toward others who are undergoing hardship. Through the years, many have told me their feelings about how badly they feel about those treated terribly, i.e., African Americans, Native Americans, the poor, prisoners, immigrants, etc.

Built into us is the desire for justice. However, it is a double-edged sword because that desire can bring strong emotions when justice doesn't happen as we want in a situation. Compassion, sympathy, and empathy require considering all parties of a problem—those who perpetrate unkind and vicious things to others and those who want to correct it.

There is evil in the world, and the challenge is how to deal with it. We can stay resentful and maintain a heavy protective armor or do all we can to prevent its harmful effects. It is ideal to let go of its harmful effects and still advocate against it without fear. Sadly, it is interesting to note that one side in disputes including politics, often considers the opposing side evil and/or the enemy.

To maintain my peace of mind and joy, anytime I judge another, which is frequently, I stop myself and work on forgiving instead. To maintain goodwill toward people, those who feel for others, who have empathy, compassion, and sympathy, need to cultivate the skill of letting go of upsets toward those who disagree with their perspective. He or she can then think more clearly about how to help or make a positive difference in their area of influence versus simply spewing out anger. That's a choice we always have, but I understand that this is a challenge.

Journal Exercise

1.   If you haven't done this already, write down all the situations in your city, country, and the world that upsets you. (This is important because people often avoid big situations because those events are too big to deal with. However, we know that this just means we need to break down the problem even more.)

2.   Who and what do you think is the cause of your upset? Be specific. Put down as many people and factors that you can think of. If it's an organization or government, put down who it is that is causing it. Keep breaking it down.

3.   Go through each of these again to identify any other factors causing your upset.

4.   Now you have a better list to work on forgiving using the tool we have already gone over, with more tools to come.

Bullying

Bullying affects one in three US children and is a significant public health problem worldwide.[1] For this reason, it is vital to address it because many adults have been the effect of bullying as a child in some way, either as direct recipients or onlookers.

Bullies and victims are at risk for negative short and long-term consequences such as depression, anxiety, low self-esteem, and delinquency.[2] Dealing with bullying with forgiveness is very helpful.

Bullying is:

1. repeated, intentional physical, verbal, or psychological attack or intimidation, with the intent to cause fear and/or harm to the victim.

2. committed by a more powerful person or group against a less powerful victim.[3]

The Health Impact of Adult Bullying In America

A survey of over 2,000 U.S. adults found 31% of Americans have been bullied as adults at a rate similar to adolescents. It is often done in the workplace, home, and educational settings. The adult victims reported substantial negative impacts on their health. The poll found:

- 70% experience anxiety/depression; 55% report a loss of confidence,
- 39% suffer from sleep loss; 26% have headaches.
- 22% experience muscle tension or pain; 19% reported a mental breakdown,
- 17% noted an inability to function day-to-day, i.e., calling in sick frequently,
- Other symptoms include gastrointestinal changes, elevated blood pressure, and cardiovascular issues.

As part of the above report, Psychiatrist Charles Sophy discloses that adult bullies are more subtle and sophisticated than children, especially using "gaslighting," which causes the victim to question their memory, judgment, and abilities. He recommends patients review common bullying tactics to identify and understand what is going on, to challenge the perpetrator, or to make an official complaint. [4]

What Bullies do

Here is a list from research collected by Pediatric researcher Rashmi Shetgiri MD that describes what a child might have gone through or tacitly let happen, which can cause guilt: [5]

- Physical bullying = Hitting, pushing, kicking, choking, forcefully taking something from the victim
- Verbal bullying = Name-calling, threatening, taunting, malicious teasing, psychological intimidation using words.

- Relational bullying = Gossiping, slandering, sabotage, convincing peers to exclude victims
- Cyberbullying = Using an electronic medium for threatening, harassing, taunting, and intimidating. Some of the methods used are:
  o sending cruel or threatening messages,
  o taking over the victims' email account and sending embarrassing or vicious messages to others that appear as if they have come from the victim,
  o creating websites with pictures or jokes about victims and inviting other classmates to participate in ridiculing victims online, and
  o tricking victims into revealing sensitive information through email or instant messaging and then forwarding it to others.

The effect of cyberbullying can be devastating because:

- The victim might not know who is bullying them or why because cyberbullying can happen anonymously.
- Cyberbullying can have a large audience.
- Cruelty is easier using technology because the bullies might not see the serious harm from their actions because they can't see the victim's response.
- Managing cyberbullying by parents and adults is harder.

Cyber bullied kids report feeling depressed, sad, angry, frustrated, lack of confidence, worthless, fear of going to school, and suicidal.[6]

A major study shows two out of five young adults have been cyberbullied and that adults can be *worse* than teenagers when it comes to virtual harassment.[7]

Dr. Walser deLara, a Social Worker, interviewed more than 800 people age 18 - 65 about the lasting effects of bullying. In her book, *Bullying Scars*, she reports that her research showed that years after people were bullied, many still struggled with trust and self-esteem, developed psychiatric problems, and relied on food, alcohol, or drugs to cope.[8]

Characteristics of Bullies As Children

Better understanding the bully will help in the forgiving process. Research reveals some of the typical characteristics of bullies: dominant personalities, boys more than girls, defiant behaviors, drug use, plus they often deal with one or more of these conditions- ADHD, depression, oppositional/ conduct disorder [9]

Bullies often come from homes where there is:
- Maternal depression or decreased maternal attachment to the child
- Suboptimal maternal mental health
- Mother more likely to be irritable, critical, and hostile.
- Poor parent-child communication
- Poor parenting behaviors
- Parental anger with their child
- Parental use of corporal punishment
- Substance abuse in the home
- Living in an unsafe neighborhood [10]

As you see by the list, they don't come from healthy homes.

If you were bullied as a child, carrying that upset around can cause years of pain. To work on it with forgiveness, first, break down the upset into its smallest parts.

Here are some questions to help:
1. Who was the bully?

2. Try to see if you can understand him from the list above.

3. Who helped him or her?

4. Who watched and didn't help?

5. Who didn't help who should have?

6. Who did you feel betrayed by and perhaps turned on you?

7. Can you forgive these kids now?

The Key Question

When you break down a difficult situation, or even when working on one person, a key or essential question will usually come up in your mind about what happened to cause the trouble, such as, "What was it that made them do it?" Answering that question over and over will bring up different answers. This questioning will help you understand what happened.

One client volunteered that she had always been hurt by her father's coldness to her. She asked his friends about what he was like when he was younger and about his upbringing. When she knew the facts about her father's childhood, she could forgive him. It often takes time and sincere effort to delve deeply into a situation or the other person's history.

A Technique to Make Forgiveness Go Faster – Look Earlier

Looking at earlier upsets or events like the present one helps resolve a string of similar experiences. Why? Because each new experience we have attaches itself to an already- formed group of similar experiences in our brain, [11, 12, 13] which we talked of in chapter 7.

If you are still having difficulty forgiving someone, ask these questions:

1. Has someone done this same or similar hurt to me at an earlier time?

2. Have you done this or something similar earlier in your life to another?

3. Have you been in this situation before? If so, find and look at the earlier time. Find who it was and what they did to you, and what you did to them.

4. If you are still having difficulty, ask yourself if there is an even earlier time, this situation occurred. For example, an upset with husband #2 might be like one with husband #1, and possibly earlier with Mom or Dad.

5. If your view of the upset doesn't change much, you might look even earlier.

6. You can also break the current one down into more manageable parts and check if you experienced one or all those similar parts at an earlier time.

The Overlooked Aid for Help - Outside Support

Often, we try to do things by our self. If you find that your stress reactions have imprisoned you, seek outside help. Talking things out with someone else can help get your feet back on the ground and return to the forgiveness routine. An "outside" person like a therapist or someone you respect can sometimes see the larger emotional patterns more quickly than you because they are outside the issue, not trapped by it.

Also, read other forgiveness books, articles, or videos. We recommend the books and videos of forgiveness researchers Dr. Robert Enright, Dr. Evert Worthington, Dr. Fred Luskin, and Dr. Michael McCullough, to name a few.

In my psychotherapy training, we learned that the client will often bring in our own issues, so therapists often have supervisors or mentors to help the therapist. Likewise, your family member or friend might bring in your forgiveness issues. By dealing with your issues and problems, you will find that you will help them more effectively.

Speaking with a social worker, a therapist, minister, priest, rabbi, teacher, or even a trusted family member or friend can help. But be careful not to seek their help to support you in holding onto your upsets.

1. Is there a trusted friend, therapist, etc., you can talk with to help in your situation, someone who will remain objective?

2. Decide how to proceed together.

Notes

Chapter 12
The Long-Term Effects of Stress and Dealing with It Effectively

I hope that you don't need this chapter. I have it because a larger amount of people than we think are dealing with stress for years. It is my hope that the information in this chapter might be helpful to them and to you who might be concerned about a friend or relative's situation.

It includes a very useful letters process that students have had very good results from.

The Signs of Stress Overload and Exhaustion

Research shows that the chemicals and hormones the body releases during stress can have the following effects on us:

- Open us up to cancer, chronic infections, and disease.

- Lead to ulcers, swelling, pain, tenderness in joints, and asthma.

- Weaken the circulatory system, leading to strokes, heart disease, heart attack, and high blood pressure.

- And they may cause depression or aggression.[1]

There is even evidence that intense psychological stress can change the brain's makeup, perhaps permanently.[1a]

The Consequences of Long-Term Stress

When the stress system chronically dominates a person's life, serious health problems can result, including

- Mental health problems, such as depression, anxiety, and personality disorders
- Obesity and other eating disorders
- Menstrual problems

- Skin and hair problems, such as acne, psoriasis, and eczema, and permanent hair loss
- Gastrointestinal problems, such as GERD, gastritis, ulcerative colitis, and irritable colon
- For adults—Cardiovascular disease, including heart disease, high blood pressure, abnormal heart rhythms, heart attacks, and stroke.[2]

Management by Fear

When people are constantly belittled, criticized, and discredited, their fear can make them begin to believe those condemnations are true, even when they are experienced and competent adults.[3]

Research from the University of Minnesota tells us that once fear pathways are activated, the brain bypasses more rational processing paths and reacts defensively. In this overactive state, the brain perceives events as negative and remembers them that way going forward.[4] Thus, fear keeps a person stressed, preventing them from using their entire brain to develop viable solutions.

To avoid being controlled by base brain areas, a person must be willing to look at their behavior as an observer would—as if it were not their own.[5] The whole idea of mindfulness is exactly this, and why there are so many exercises.

From a detached perspective, you can ask yourself questions to understand what might be creating your reactions. It's essential to maintain an objective viewpoint with yourself or for someone you might be helping. This is the basis of good therapy.

Questions to ask yourself:
a. Who, if anyone, has tried to control you through fear, threats, and constant pressure?

b. Write down the person's name and what he/she did.

c. Write down the effect they had on you.

d. Now, look at how you behaved in that situation.

e. Do your forgiveness work on these situations.

Burnout

When stress is chronic, it may easily lead to burnout, which is a state of emotional, mental, and often physical exhaustion brought on by prolonged or repeated stress.[6] I believe it is essential to be aware of burnout symptoms to take care of yourself and seek help. Here are the signs to be aware of:

- Emotional, mental, and physical exhaustion
- Sleep disruptions
- Headaches, stomach aches, body aches
- Susceptibility to colds and flu[7]

To prevent burnout, tell your friends how you're feeling. It works. In a study of student nurses doing emotionally taxing work in a life-or-death environment, those who could do two things were less prone to burnout.

1) Draw on support from friends and colleagues,

2) Genuinely expressing their emotions—from sorrow to frustration to joy.

Those students were better able to continue the tough emotional work their job required.[8]

Being A Victim of Negative Situations

Truths about our seeming lack of control in situations are:

a. We continually make decisions and choices.

b. Our decisions often affect what happens to us.

When we realize that adverse reactions are going on inside us, we can take control and seek help.

These are only a few of the questions for you:

1. Where in your life do you feel you are a victim of someone or situation?

2. What self-forgiveness can you do so that you feel better?

3. Are there any apologies to be made by you?

4. How can you take care of yourself and feel safe?

5. What limits do you need to set on yourself and the other?

To look more in-depth at constant victimization in your life, here are some questions and directions to help:

Here are questions concerning your perceived lack of control:

1. What choices did I make that resulted in this situation?

2. What decisions did I make?

3. What decisions can I make now to change it?

Protection Against Victimization

When the children have the characteristics of a victim but have more friends and protective peer relationships, they can be protective against victimization by a bully. However, suppose the child does not have close friends and has low supportiveness and protection. In that case, they are more likely to experience rejection and isolation by peers and be victimized by bullies because they see them as an easy target.[9] Kids with good friends are not easy targets because their friends will be protective unless their friends also fit the same risk factors. Interestingly, research also shows that teachers' warm and caring behavior towards all students is also protective against child victimization.[10] With this in mind, I believe adults could try the same recommendations if they are being bullied.

Trauma's Longer-Term Consequences

You may have had what is called "tolerable stress," like the death of a loved one, divorce of parents, or natural disaster. In this, the body's alert systems are activated to a greater degree but are time-limited and cushioned by other caring people.

With stress, you might see:

- Phobias, general anxiety (especially in natural disaster survivors)

- Depression or guilt

- Psychosomatic complaints

- An altered sense of time

- Grief reactions and obsessions with death, especially among those who survived a trauma in which someone died or could have died

- Increased interpersonal conflicts and outbursts of anger

- Absenteeism and truancy[11]

Brain imaging studies by Bessel A. Van der Kolk, MD, noted international trauma specialist, tell us that the part of the brain not associated with language shows the most activity during a traumatic event. This indicates that the front part of the brain associated with speech and talking about events shuts off during trauma.[12]

When a trauma victim does eventually "speak," it may be with the voice of rage. This means that people don't always need to talk about trauma to resolve it, but work on quieting their bodies down. Thus, Dr.

Van der Kolk recommends that both adults and teens do physical activities like tai chi, yoga, dancing, and breathing to calm themselves. Licensed therapists can treat patients using EMDR (Eye Movement Desensitization And Reprocessing) therapy,[13, 14] an effective method to help people resolve fear and problems through eye movement.

A similar approach that anyone can try is called EFT--Emotional Freedom Technique or tapping. It is easy to use, has no undesirable side effects, and is empowering. EMDR and EFT have been used successfully in forgiving.

How and Why Self-Forgiveness Helps with Trauma

You can prevent traumatic incidents from being harmful by forgiving your mistakes, especially if you feel guilty about a traumatic experience and are saying negative things against yourself. "If only" and "I should have" statements are ineffective because they are continually focusing on the negative. To forgive yourself is urgent. To get your mind out of the rut of obsessively attacking yourself, try doing the Lovingkindness Blessing for others and yourself. There are plenty of methods to help in the book.

I appreciate this joke because it hits so close to the craziness of self-condemnation:

From the Management: The beatings will continue until morale improves!

Trauma and Forgiveness

Remember that forgiveness has a timing all its own. If a person is in the middle of reacting to a terrible event, forcing forgiveness will not work and might upset the person more. Initially, a person who is still reacting might need to use stress-reduction methods like meditation, relaxation, massage, walks, and perhaps psychotherapy.

The Letters Practice

This forgiveness practice is one of the most effective that I have found to help my students forgive difficult people in their lives. It is one of the best you can do at any time to help in forgiving.

Write these letters in sequence.

NOTE: If several people are involved in your upset, write a separate letter sequence for each person.

I. The Hurt Letter

1. Write a letter to the person you want to forgive. Vent all your feelings, emotions, and thoughts. Write down everything that hurts you, that you find unforgivable, and everything that robs you of the strength and willingness to consider forgiving. (You can even draw an emotional picture of the upset.)

2. Do you experience embarrassment, humiliation, or shame?

3. Are you willing to look at these feelings and not avoid them?

4. Repeat the steps above for other similar events that have happened with this same person. Include all of this in your letter.

5. Keep going until you have nothing left to say. (I remember one person drew the person's face and then scribbled all over it with different crayons.)

6. Now put this letter aside

7. Take a break if you need to.

II. The Response Letter

1. Now write a second letter—the response. Write it from the offender's point of view, as if it came from him or her.

2. Answer each of your upsets from the perspective of what you think the offender would say.

3. Include the offender's explanations or justifications of how they were affected by your grief or upset.

4. Include an apology if you want one.

5. If you want your offender to have a positive insight about you, include it as well.

6. You may find several things happening during this exercise. Journal what you see and feel.

I learned from doing hypnotherapy that including the offender's reaction (even though you are writing it from wishful thinking), the mind often sees it as real.

Please note: To truly understand a person's world view, walk in their shoes.

"Walk in Their Shoes" Journal exercise

1. What do you believe is this person's governing moral code? Should it have influenced their behavior differently?

2. How do they see the world? What do they fear and love, like and dislike?

3. What was it like growing up in their family?

4. What were his or her issues?

5. What is their emotional intelligence?

6. What was the person's expectation of you?

7. Keep going until you feel a shift in awareness.

If you can't answer these questions, then you do not know enough to condemn this person.

III. The Gratitude Letter

1. Now write a letter of appreciation to the person you wish to forgive.

2. Include your thankfulness for their contribution(s) to your life. As you write, release your negative feelings about the person as they do not belong in this letter. Journal them as they come up.

3. Thank them for the gifts you have received from them over the years.

4. Tell them, if you can, how you matured mentally, emotionally, or spiritually from doing this forgiveness activity.

5. Thank them for what you have learned from them. Express your appreciation for who they have been in your life.

6. If there was ever love between you and the individual, pretend to feel this love and remember what you once loved about the person.

7. Appreciate their positive qualities and write down what you admire about them.

8. Include how they inspired you.

9. Speak of the love given and love received.

10. Include an apology if you have caused the person upset or harm.

11. Notice any shift in your body. Write down your insights.

    NEVER send the first two letters—they are only for your healing. However, you might consider sending your gratitude letter.

    NOTE: If it is still too hard to write the gratitude letter, then hold off until appropriate. Never rush your forgiveness actions; you will know when you are ready to move on.

12. What thoughts, feelings, and issues has this exercise brought to mind?

    (A portion of the Gratitude letter comes from the *Honorable Closure* work[15] of Dr. Angeles Arrien, a cultural anthropologist and award-winning author. I highly recommend her many books for anyone interested in what is common to us across religions and cultures.)

Notes

Chapter 13
Summary of Working on Upsets

This Chapter contains an organized summary of the forgiveness actions given in preceding chapters so that you don't have to go searching through the book for the methods to use. It contains the entire Power Forgiveness Approach, which includes the Secrets and Basics we went over in chapter 10. I have broken the Approach into steps for better understanding and clarity.

Use the points in this chapter as a checklist in your work on forgiving.

An Overview of Power Forgiveness

As I mentioned in the first part of the book, forgiving involves different steps to take with each situation that you address. Sometimes you will go through them quickly, while other situations will take more time.

Forgiveness is a process—a series of actions, each having a set of steps that leads to viewing a challenging situation in a different, more beneficial way. It is the art of moving the mind toward being more open, happy, and accepting of others and self. Often, forgiving will not be effective until there is understanding and compassion. Once these are experienced, forgiveness might automatically follow, or the decision to forgive becomes easier so that healing can occur.

Digging deeply into a situation with an understanding of how the mind operates can make the decision to forgive easier. It can take time. How long is entirely up to you.

Once I decided to forgive and committed myself to the process, I worked on forgiving all of my upsets in one long sitting until I felt complete. Others find that it works better to take many sessions over a more extended period. The length of time does not matter as long as you follow the *Power Forgiveness Approach* I outline here. Sometimes, I copy these steps to use them in an hour-long session. I run people through the steps to the point that they 1) release each upset, 2) do self-forgiveness on that upset, and then 3) give gratitude toward the offender. If there is time, we take another upset and do the same actions to treat another upset.

The *Power Forgiveness Approach* Outline:
- Step I - Open the heart and mind to the upset and expand your understanding and compassion. This extensive step also includes Skillful Actions to help you.
- Step II – Realize Forgiveness – For each successful forgiveness, there is a realization or shift in perspective or attitude. This step ensures that full forgiveness has occurred.
- Step III – Gain Self-Forgiveness -- This step ensures that your forgiveness work remains complete for what you just forgave by the offender.
- Step IV - Give thanks for the healing and feeling gratitude for what was learned from the offender and situation.
- Repeat steps I-IV until all resentments, anger, grudges, hurts, and betrayals you can think of are forgiven.

Make sure you look through your journal to make sure all upsets are covered. As you look in the journal, ask yourself, for example: "How do you feel about that problem with your brother using your clothes?" If the upset is still there, continue working on step I. If you were to say, "yeh, it's fine," you still need to move through Steps II to IV.

You might not need to address each part of Step I. You might completely forgive somewhere along the way in Step I. In that case, there would be no reason to go through the later parts of Step I or the Skillful Actions for Understanding and Compassion. You would move directly to Step II to ensure the forgiveness is complete, and then to Step III and IV.

Step I – Unlocking an Upset and Expanding Understanding and Compassion

Start here to work on an upset. Use these actions and skills that each time you deal with a person or a situation. From your list of upsets:

1. Make a choice that starts small and feels right.

Start small. Take one upset, or even part of one, to work on. You might be working with one person out of a group of people or with one of many upsets with one person. Make sure you break down the upset into bite-size pieces.

2. Look at Willingness.

Ask yourself: Are you willing to work on this upset? If not, choose another upset. Sometimes initially, you might think you want to deal with something but then realize you don't. Willingness is essential because it provides the beginning of the commitment that leads to forgiving.

3. Focus on what inspires you to forgive that offending person or situation

Always make sure you have a worthy reason, inspiration, and motivation when you do forgiving work. Start each forgiving period with something that inspires you about forgiving. It might be something general in the offender's life or something specific about them. Then carry it through.

4. Deal with feelings effectively

Ask: What do you feel when you think of the emotional situation? (Dealing with emotions is valuable to prevent false forgiveness.)

Journal:
1. What do I feel when I think of the person involved in this situation? For example, sad, depressed, angry, apathetic, guilty, hurt, anxious.

2. Apart from my primary emotion, when I think of this situation, are there other feelings underneath or mixed up with the main one, like embarrassment, humiliation, or shame?

3. Am I willing to engage these feelings and not avoid them?

4. What was I afraid would happen at the time? What am I afraid of now if I forgive?

5. Find Needs and Debts Owed

Remember, our working definition of forgiveness is letting go of what you feel the offender owes you. Ask:

1. What does the other person owe you for having to feel what you have felt?

2. What do you need out of the situation? What would satisfy you?

Here are further questions to help you in this step:

a. Am I willing to entertain the possibility of not getting what I think the person owes me?

b. Is it worth carrying this upset when it is unrealistic that I will ever get what I want from him or her?

c. Can I let it go to gain peace of mind?

6. Look at the real consequences of holding onto this upset

This step does not have to be an essay; it can be done in a few moments.

Answer and journal about:

A. The Payoff:

1. What do I get by keeping the upset going? Write down any benefits. Who benefits and how?

2.	Is being right more important than being happy?

B. **Negative consequences of holding onto an upset:**
Sometimes you don't notice how much an upset has affected you. If so, consider these questions:

1.	What am I getting out of this upset? List the negatives.

2.	What is happening to the people closest to me by my holding onto the upset?

3.	How happy am I in my life?

4.	Could letting go of this situation increase love, peace, and joy in my life?

C. **Being a Victim:**
1.	How long has my victimization been going on?

2.	How long is it okay to let others be in control of my happiness?

3.	Am I a possible contributor to the problem and not just the victim?

7. Address the Resistance to Forgiving- Make sure no Myths of Forgiveness are active.

Misunderstandings about the nature of forgiveness often prevent people from forgiving. If these are affecting your progress, re-read the section on Myths of Forgiveness in Chapter 2.

8. Decide to Forgive:
More questions to answer:

1. Can I decide to forgive right now so that I feel better?

2. Even though he/she doesn't deserve it, can I forgive as an act of compassion toward the other person and myself?

As you decide to forgive, keep going through the rest of the stages. Forgiving someone is not the end of this work. If you want to be rid of the situation for good, forgive yourself too, which is **Step III.**

NOTE: The more you decide to forgive and feel the resulting emotional relief, the easier it will be to decide to forgive at another time. The Power Forgiveness process speeds up as you repeat the steps because the decision to forgive will require less effort.

Skillful Actions for Step I - to Use for Expanding Understanding and Compassion

Here are questions to ask yourself.

Skillful Action 1: Assess your Rules of Conduct:

1. Which of your principles did the offender not follow?

2. Which of your values were rejected or disregarded?

3. What rules did they break?

4. With each rule, principle, and value, ask the following:

- Is my expectation realistic given his or her life experience?

- Have I always followed these principles and rules myself?

- Have I done the same/similar thing to others? Or myself?

Skillful Action 2: Change Your Perspective:

"When you, as the victim, can begin to understand the limitations of your victimizer, you can also begin to recognize his humanity." Terry Hargrave, Ph.D [1]

◆ **Walk in the Other's Shoes:**

1. Write down what you believe to be the governing moral code that this person lives by, and that should have influenced their behavior in this situation.

2. Write down what you believe were their fears and hopes, likes, and dislikes.

3. What was it like growing up in their family?

4. What was it like to come from their culture or time?

5. What are their issues?

6. What is their emotional intelligence?

7. What was their expectation of you, of others?

    If you don't have enough information about the person, ask someone who may —if that someone exists, is available and willing.

♦   **What is the big picture?**
   1. Write down how this situation might fit your idea of Karma or a Divine Plan (if those are important or mean anything to you.)

   2. Was this person in your life to teach you a valuable lesson?

♦   **Other questions for changing perspectives**
   1. Sign a contract.

   2. What are other ways that I could see this situation?

   3. Am I willing to listen to others who might have a different viewpoint?

   4. Am I willing to get help from others?

5. How would an impartial observer look at this?

6. What have I left out? Have I skipped over anything where I may have contributed to the wrong outcome?

7. Am I holding onto this resentment out of loyalty to someone else?

For completing Skillful Action #2:

- Ensure you have addressed all the ways that the offender is correct and justified from their perspective.

- Be sure to pay attention to the felt shifts in your perspectives and feelings during this stage.

Skillful Action 3 – Facing Defenses

As we have discussed earlier, we often push wrongs we have done out of our minds and/or the responsibility for the wrong onto others. When we deny that we did that wrong action, and we defend ourselves by being hurt or indignant, we maintain our self-image by blaming what happens to us on others.

Questions to see if you are projecting:

1. How would an impartial observer view this?

2. What have I added that I should not have?

<u>Facing Defenses Summary Questions</u> - Journal your answers

a. How would an impartial observer view this?

b. Have I done something similar (not in magnitude but context) to others and/or myself?

c. If yes, can I forgive this person for doing the same thing I've done? Or for breaking an unrealistic value, moral code, or rule that I have?

d. Can I forgive myself for doing the same thing?

Skillful Action 4 – Work with Ways to Feel More Positive.
♦ <u>Find a deeper meaning in the event</u> – Journal:
1. What has this hurtful experience taught me about myself, the world, or other people?

2. How have I matured from this experience?

3. What have I learned about love and compassion as a result of this experience?

4. How have my values changed?

◆ <u>Appreciate what you gained – be grateful!</u>
Journal:
1. Can you look for and acknowledge how the person who hurt you may have helped you too?

2. Do you intend to thank those who have taught you major life lessons?

3. What could you gain from asking yourself, "What am I thankful for from this situation?

◆ <u>Give love</u>:
1. Could you hold or hug the person in your mind that you are trying to forgive and love them no matter what, like a mother or father embracing their child? You might still disagree, but no longer with a closed heart. Working on this might produce a felt-shift inside you. Notice what changes for you.

2. If you forgave, go to the next piece in the broken-down situation.

>>If you were unable to forgive the person, break the hurt down further. Then go through the steps on the newly broken-down upset.
<u>OR</u>, look back further and ask these questions:
1. Is there an earlier situation in my life that might be similar to this one?

2. What do I need to let go of in my past and my family of origin to help me?

3. How else could I view this situation?

4. Can I get help from others? Are there others I might talk with who have a different perspective?

5. Be silent, and give your unforgiven situation to the intuition you have. Be aware of a response. Have faith and love. Remember to ask for Inner Help to see the situation differently. You have done all you can.

>>If there is no change, take another incident, work on it with Step I, and return to this upset later.

>> If at any point as you are working on the Skillful Actions, you feel good about the person or situation, go to Step II below - **Realize Forgiveness** to make sure the forgiveness is complete.

As I said in Principle VIII (see Chapter 11), momentum builds as one forgives. After a while, the questions in the steps might take only a little time, perhaps just a few seconds to answer. Here are examples for Step I – Unlocking an Upset and Expanding Understanding and Compassion

1. Make a choice that feels right. Yep

2. Look at Willingness. Yep!

3. Focus on what inspires you to forgive that person or situation Yep

4. Deal with feelings effectively a) angry and hurt, b) embarrassed, c) yep, d) she would never talk to me. Forgive? Not yet.

5. <u>Find Needs and Debt Owed</u>

a) The embarrassment I felt. b) An apology in front of everyone.

a. Yes, b. No, it isn't, c. Yes, I can forgive her!!!!

That would be the end of that upset. Continue to Step II to make sure.

In Step II, as long as there was a felt-shift or probably a smile or realization, you would proceed directly to Steps III and IV. When Step IV is done, start on a new upset with a new Step I. Sometimes you might have to go through every part of Step I and the Skillful Actions to deal with a situation or person.

After a while, I have found that most people know and understand the routine and resolve the issue/resentment pretty quickly. These steps don't have to take lots of explaining.

Step II – Realize Forgiveness

This step is to ensure your forgiveness in Step I is complete.

For each successful forgiveness, you will:

1. Experience a positive shift in your perspective and attitude about the situation or offender.
2. Have positive feelings for the offender.

Take the time to feel the change within. Think of the person again to see if there is any resentment or hurt left, and whether there are positive feelings toward the offender.

>> If 1. And 2. Are strong, go to Step III

>> If you do not fully experience 1. and 2. (directly above), even though you might have experienced a felt-shift in Step I, there is more to forgive about the offender, which means you would go back to Step I -The Understanding Step to continue dealing with that offender, probably by breaking down the upset more.

Step III – Gain Self-Forgiveness

This step is built on what was just forgiven in the offender in Step II. Ask yourself the following questions concerning the offender you just addressed. Completing this step ensures that your forgiveness work remains complete.

Self-forgiveness questions:

1. Is this unforgiven situation mirroring something about me?

2. Have I done anything comparable to myself or others? (The magnitude might not be the same, but is there a similarity?)

3. Can I forgive myself for the same offense for which I have forgiven another?

4. Do I feel guilt surrounding my transgression, for which I need to forgive myself?

5. What will it take me to forgive myself for this? Do I need to make amends to anyone?

6. This question might help those with a Christian orientation: Can I accept God's forgiveness for doing this deed?

When you feel you have forgiven yourself for the same act you forgave the other, you will naturally flow to the next stage to complete the work on this upset.

Remember, I'm not saying the offense is exactly the same, but it might be. We are talking of metaphorical thinking here. The question is, "How does their action apply to me. And can I forgive myself for that?"

Step IV - Thanksgiving - The Healing
Journal Exercise
1. What can I be grateful for in this situation? What did it teach me?

2. Did it make me stronger, more capable, or successful?

3. What did I learn?

4. How did the person or people help me?

5. How have they helped others?

6. How did they affect a positive change in my life?

Continue selecting situations that bother you. Repeat Steps I-IV of the Approach, returning to the Healing step each time until there is nothing left to forgive.

Notes

Chapter 14
Continued Healing & Its Results

Chapter 14 addresses how to keep yourself open to forgiving and make it part of your daily life.

The first part of the chapter has a basic summary of what we have gone over previously. It does not include the questions I asked. These are just basic principles, and after those, actions that make a difference. The complete approach for Power Forgiveness was in Chapter 13. These are the principles, secrets and essentials behind our Steps to Complete Forgiveness.

In the back of the book, for your convenience in APPENDIX C, you will find 24 Forgiveness Methods called Working In-depth with the Forgiving Ways ~ CPR For Forgiving ~ Ways to Breathe Healing into Your Life. It summarizes many of the forgiveness methods I spoke of throughout the book, broken down into three categories—Communication, Perspective, and Responsibility.

Part A

The Principles, Secrets, and Essentials Behind the Steps

The Principles of Power Forgiveness

Here are what I feel are principles or values for Power Forgiveness, which is letting all upsets go—all resentments, guilt, desire for revenge, anger, hate, grudges, etc., with everyone, anywhere, at any time.

1. Forgiveness is a re-examination of self and others in a different light and is a movement of the heart that opens one up to be more compassionate, kind, and loving.

2. With true forgiveness, there is a positive attitude toward the offending person.

3. Keep motivation and willingness high when forgiving. Focusing on one's highest purpose or vision will allow forgiveness to take place. Focus on what inspires you to forgive.

4. Commit to forgiving. 1. Be willing to forgive. 2. Intend to forgive. 3. Do it—forgive.

5. Keep feelings in view while forgiving. Look for the feelings under the surface. Avoiding difficult feelings is normal but not helpful in this work. You cannot let go of something hidden.

6. Letting go of negatives perspectives and feelings will bring about the profound positive change desired. Negative feelings take the mind in opposite directions from love, joy, and peace.

7. Momentum builds as one forgives, and the inner work speeds up because the mind starts to be less burdened by unforgiveness and will feel more relaxed and even love the good results.

8. Stop the process anytime to de-escalate stress. Fight, flight, freeze, and hide reactions prevent forgiving.

9. Always break down an upset as far as you can.

10. Find the metaphor, representation, or symbol in the upset. It is how the mind works, i.e., the boss may represent dad, or the wife as mom.

11. Find Forgiveness for Yourself. Forgiveness becomes permanent when you forgive yourself for the same thing for which you have forgiven another. You will no longer need to project your upset with yourself onto others to protect and feel good about yourself.

12. Reaction to our outer world reflects our inner ones.

13. Be grateful. Anytime that you can be thankful to a person or about a situation, you change it. At the end of any forgiving, find gratitude. What did you gain from the situation? For what can you be grateful to that person?

14. Love is the key. Love is for giving.

The Secrets in Doing this Work

For 50 years, I have done a wide range of counseling work, including that of forgiveness. Throughout these years, I found the following counseling wisdom to be significant in helping people forgive. Because so few people, in general, are aware of these steps, I call them Secrets. They are:

- **Be compassionate.** Look at the other person's perspective to understand another's situation and world view—walk in their shoes.

- **Break down the Situation.** Analyze it piece by piece, person by person. Break down big upsets by listing everything the offender has done. Break down an upset or resentments with an organization by listing all the people who represent that organization. As you think of one, others will come to mind.

- **Look for Earlier Events.** Search for past experiences that are the same or similar to the one you are working on now. The brain works by building on memories that are already there. Therefore, deal with earlier people and situations in your life when you are not able to forgive someone in the present. Appreciation of life deepens as we mend the upsets with our family, religion, and culture of origin.

- **Use Imagination** to calm you and to look at your offender differently.

- **Ask for Inner Help** when you are not sure what to do or how to understand something. Be silent, offer it to your intuition, and listen. The more you ask and listen, the more faith you will have in your intuition.

- **Be aware of The Small Shifts of Heart and Attitude**—With each act of forgiving, you should feel a change inside—the felt-shift.
  - o   Pay attention to your body during forgiveness work. Notice shifts in major muscle groups or changes in breathing or body language
  - o   Watch for realization or an "Ahhh," and relief, perhaps a smile.

o   Pay attention to your energy levels and take breaks as you feel you need.

o   Notice shifts in perspective and understanding; that is the Aha! Response.

A Review of the Essential of Forgiveness

The above "secrets" are really part of the basics or essentials of the activities and processes of forgiving that I feel are crucial in doing this work. Here are more basics.

You can use this list and the secrets above as a checklist when you are doing your forgiveness work:

- **Get a commitment to do this work.** The best way is to fill out a contract like the one in Chapter 4, Page 57, to assist with their commitment.

- **Write, talk about, draw**, etc., what is going on now or about a specific subject or person.

- **Work with the easiest upsets first**, not the most difficult ones.

- **Chose a comfortable, safe, non-threatening environment** to work in.

- **Acknowledging that you have done a similar thing to another** will many times bring about a release occur.

- **Seek help from others**. Their impartial view can move forgiving forward more quickly and easily.

- **Know your values and beware of judgments**.

- **Try to make some progress each day.** Working with emotions can be tiring; go slowly if you need to, do shorter sessions, or take more breaks.

- **Find the truth. Be honest. Let go of being right.** The truth will set you free! When the truth is known, healing occurs. Honesty with ourselves is of paramount importance to our health and well-being. Defensiveness will prevent the reality of the situation from being seen and felt. Try to look at the situation as an observer would.

Part B

What to Do After You Feel Good and Don't Feel Anyone Else Needs Forgiving.

Maintaining This Work

By applying the principles, secrets, and essentials you reach the point of: **Feeling good and don't feel anyone else needs forgiving.**

To maintain the benefits of forgiveness and strengthen them, remember several key actions:

- Stay inspired for forgive,

- Find inner and outer support,

- Use in-depth tools for further forgiveness when needed, and

- Keep a regular practice.

Exercise for Maintain a Regular Practice

Maintaining a regular practice of forgiveness is the most effective way to succeed in this work and to release upsets that arise quickly.

- The best way is through an evening review, where you mentally go over your day and clean up any accumulated upsets.

- If you find that you are having a repeated upset, see if there might be something else going on, like jealousy, etc.

- Be mindful of when you may have put on your defensive armor, getting ready to fight. Quiet your mind, become more contemplative, and connect with your source of inner strength and sources of empowerment.

Forgiveness is an act of inclusion. By forgiving, we are restoring and reclaiming the love and affection we had for them. Physically we might want to bring people back into our lives or not; that is our choice.

After Deep Change - Help Others

After forgiveness work is complete, life improves in many ways. When we feel good, we naturally want to help others. As social beings, we need to feel we are moving in a noteworthy direction—not only for us but also for the greater whole—socially, nationally, and spiritually.

Releasing yourself from the destructive cycle of reliving an injury every time you think about it will restore vast amounts of positive emotional energy into your life. Use it to do good work in the world.

Other Actions That Might Come Up or Be of Value

◆ **Re-Forgiving** - When a situation arises that you thought you had forgiven, it just means there is more work to do on it. In the world we live in, it would be very difficult to live without ever running into disturbances and upsets. When new situations occur, complete the Power Forgiveness steps on them.

◆ **Value Humor** - Humor with yourself and others increases with forgiveness, and the relief you get from forgiving will help others as well.

◆ **Beware of Old Habits of the Mind** - Even though you are transforming your mind, old neural brain patterns can still show up. You are still human.

◆ **Feed yourself with the Good and Positive** - What is the best food for your mind? To feel better more often, feed your mind more of what it needs. Peace, joy, love, appreciation, nurturing can all add to your life.

◆ **Increase Values and Strengths** -The forgiving mindset lets you engage with tragedies and trauma at a higher level so that healing can occur sooner. To me, the ultimate work is the one that lets us experience Love, Joy, and the sacredness of life. While forgiveness opens the door for this, it would benefit you to develop many other qualities besides forgiveness once you have opened the door to forgiving. Positive Psychology emphasizes the importance of faith, optimism, hope, resilience, emotional intelligence, spirituality, self-affirmation, happiness, quality of life, and social support, in addition to forgiveness.

♦ **Stay Inspired** - Make it part of your practice daily to read inspirational materials that keep aligned with your highest vision. Associate with like-minded people.

♦ **Keep Forgiving** - As you forgive more and more, you become a "forgiving person" instead of a person who uses forgiveness.

♦ **Give Support – Help People Forgive** - The most powerful way to maintain a forgiving attitude is to teach it. Recommend that others forgive and help them do it. We have the tools to do it. The Forgiveness Foundation is here to help.

Reconciliation Possibilities

If it occurs in a relationship, reconciliation can feel like a blessing, but forgiveness does not always lead there. The person you had a problem with may be deceased, no longer in your life, or simply not open to a relationship with you. In such cases, reconciliation will not be possible.

After doing your forgiveness work, if you desire reconciliation, there are many books to choose from. I know and recommend these two:

♦ *Forgive for Love: The Missing Ingredient for a Healthy and Lasting Relationship,* by Fredric Luskin, Ph.D.;

♦ For Christians, Part Three of *Forgiving and Reconciling: Bridges to Wholeness and Hope,* by Dr. Everett Worthington.

This ability to let go and reconcile is not solely human. This desire for reconciliation after an altercation is noted by researchers in mammals, primates, and dolphins.[1]

The ideal of the spiritual movement in Japan, Seicho-NO-IE, is to be reconciled with everyone. As the founder said:

"True reconciliation cannot be achieved by patience or forbearance with one another. To be patient or forbearing is not to be reconciled from the bottom of your heart. When you are grateful to one another, true reconciliation is achieved."[2]

The Ultimate Result

The ultimate result of a forgiving state of mind is:

♦ Controlling our upsets, not the other way around.

- Having the humility and humanity not to resent people or God when bad things happen to us.

- Retaining a love of life and Spirit.

- Maintaining a state of mind characterized by great compassion and understanding for family, neighbor, and self.

I believe these capacities are in each of us because love, peace, and joy are available to each of us.

The Act of Forgiving - A Summary - The Hope for Humankind

The best in you comes forward in a calm, unthreatened state of mind, which allows your brain to synchronize – making sense of your life and giving meaning to your actions. Forgiveness stabilizes the mind and heart, enabling us to function at our highest level and fulfill our deepest dreams.

Forgiveness brings the mind and heart's highest function to the forefront, assisting you in letting go of unreasonable expectations, fears, and desire to harm. It enables you to undo the chronic brain stress reactions, like fear and fight, allowing you to reach their highest capacity.

Through a forgiving mind, you can function at a higher level of kindness, peace, problem-solving, and openness to the highest creative power available to them—a state to which humanity aspires.

By now, you should have many reasons to forgive others and worked on forgiving the people in your life and yourself. At the core, all the methods and techniques in this workbook increase awareness of what is going on inside you concerning upsets and the willingness to let them go, giving you better insight into dealing with offenses.

➢ Consider the progress you have made thus far.

A Vision For Forgiveness in The World

The result of forgiving every upset that we can is robust mental health, emotional well-being, and spiritual fulfillment. Thus, we use these actions to transform lives.

- We promote forgiveness and its benefits sufficiently so that people do not doubt the power of forgiving.

- We choose to be happy instead of being right.

- We choose to have loving relationships because we know they are more rewarding than being resentful.

- We recognize that we are the first to be healed by forgiving. We never know how it will affect another.

- We understand that without forgiveness first, there is no true reconciliation.

- We teach our children how to forgive so that they have happier lives with much less conflict.

- We allow others to be different without blaming them for those differences.

- We hold this vision for the future:

  - Friends counsel friends to forgive instead of just agreeing about how bad things are.

  - Individual and couples' counseling use many forgiving methods to help people let go of the upsets with themselves and others.

  - Schools open students' minds to construct win-win solutions through teaching communication skills, forgiveness, and conflict and anger management.

  - Clergy not only preach that forgiving is essential but teach people how to do it. They set up forgiveness workshops to enable their congregants to clear their minds and hearts to live deeper spiritual lives that can experience God.

  - Conflict Resolution programs throughout the world use forgiveness regularly. There is no real conflict resolution without the movement of the heart that forgiveness gives. Forgiving brings the capacity to hear what the other person really wants and says.

  - Anger control groups use forgiveness as an essential tool for healing.

  - Conferences on healing address forgiving as a powerful agent for health.

- Forgiveness of self and others is part of the healing process leading to less PTSD.

- Psychology holds the torch of forgiveness as a precursor to mental health.

- Law schools and medical schools teach the power of forgiving as a regular course of study.

- Judges require defendants to go to counselors or groups on forgiveness when appropriate.

- Nations ensure that their representatives and most valued negotiators are also accomplished in forgiving.

- Nations establish and promote their own Truth and Reconciliation programs to bring about healing among races, ethnic groups, and religions.

- The healing among religions and nations through forgiving brings us to a new era of non-violent, compassionate communication and interaction.

- The Forgiveness Foundation International is no longer necessary because churches, schools, universities, governments, communities, and households have taken up the cause of forgiveness.

Thank you for developing the skills to forgive. May you find more family and friends you can help to develop forgiveness skills.

Notes

APPENDIX A – Feelings

How We Are Likely to Feel When Our Needs Are Not Being Met

afraid	disappointed	frustrated	irate	resentful
aggravated	discouraged	furious	irritated	restless
agitated	disgusted	grief	jealous	sad
angry	disheartened	guilty	let-down	scared
anxious	dislike	hate	lethargy	shaky
apathetic	displeased	heavy	listless	shocked
bad	distressed	helpless	lonely	skeptical
bitter	disturbed	horrified	mad	sorry
blue	downhearted	horrible	mean	spiritless
bored	dread	hostile	miserable	surprised
brokenhearted	embarrassed	humiliated	nervous	suspicion
cold	embittered	hurt	overwhelmed	terrified
confused	exhausted	impatient	passive	troubled
dejected	fatigued	indifferent	perplexed	unhappy
depressed	fear	infuriated	puzzled	upset
despair	frightened	insecure	reluctant	worry

Feelings Likely to Be Present When Your Needs Are Being Satisfied

affection	eager	free	joyful	splendid
amazed	ecstatic	friendly	loving	surprised
appreciation	elated	fulfilled	optimism	tenderness
astonished	electrified	glad	peaceful	thankful
blissful	encouraged	glorious	pleasant	thrilled
calm	energetic	glowing	proud	tranquil
carefree	enjoyment	grateful	quiet	trust
cheerful	enthusiastic	happy	radiant	wonderful
confident	exhilarated	helpful	satisfied	
contented	expansive	hopeful	secure	
delighted	exuberant	inspired	sensitive	

Permission to use granted from *Nonviolent Communication* 3rd edition by Dr. Marshall Rosenberg, www.NonviolentCommunication.com

APPENDIX B - Empowerment

Effective Ways of Empowering Yourself and Others
Higher Beingness

1. Am I connecting to the highest aspect of myself?

2. Is there some way that I can connect with the Higher Power of my understanding?

3. What can I do to have a stronger connection with inner peace, love, hope, faith, trust & joy?

Love

1. How can I bring a more loving, compassionate, or empathetic perspective into this situation?

2. How can I gain a more open-hearted perspective about this person?

3. Can I give a gift of forgiveness to this person (though they might not deserve it)?

4. Disregarding everything else, can I flow love to this person from my heart to theirs? (Do this until you feel a change in your reaction to them. You could do this a few times a day if necessary.)

Inspiration

1. Have I taken the time to relax and contemplate the highest in myself to do this forgiveness work?

2. Can I take a moment to relax and find or ask for inspiration to assist me in forgiving?

3. Are there inspirational writings that can help me with forgiveness and my life?

Analysis

1. Am I letting my emotions get in the way?

2. Is there a more rational way to deal with this?

3. Is my logic getting in the way of what is right in this situation?

4. How would an impartial observer view this?

Support

1. What would support me in doing forgiveness work?

2. What support group could help me deal with my negative life situations to be more positive about my life?

3. How can I take care of myself better?

APPENDIX C - Working In-depth with the Forgiving Ways ~ 24 Forgiveness Methods
CPR For Forgiving
~ Ways to Breathe Healing into Your Life ~

Here is a review of some of the many processes we went over in the book. This time they are broken into ones on communication, perspective, and responsibility methods.

There is room at the back of the book for notes.

Communication

Communication often enables us to step out of an upset and achieve a better understanding of a situation. Relief occurs by communicating with others and our intuition to gain insight. Here are some communication methods you can use:

Letters of Hurt, Response, and Gratitude
See The Letters Exercise in Chapters 11.

Do not send the first two letters but consider sending the gratitude one.

Dialogue Process
Journaling a dialogue about the situation is powerful. You do this by writing about your upset and then asking yourself questions that come to mind about the situation. Fully engage your honesty and mind. When you write, start with one of the questions. You might then ask, "How could they have done this?" Then search your mind for a possible answer. Once answered, ask the next question that comes to mind. We often do this with friends when we try to understand something, allowing intuition to come forward. Then ask the next *burning* question that comes up for you.

Another version of this process is to answer the question as if the other person is answering it.

To start, ask yourself what you would most like to know about the situation you are dealing with. Any of these questions will start the process.

- Down deep, what is causing this upset?

- How can you take control of your anger, revenge, and attack thoughts?

- How can you see a different viewpoint in this situation?

Sending Love

Sending love from your heart to the person you are upset with until you feel a shift in attitude is very powerful and helpful. That would be enough for the upset to be gone. You might still disagree, but not hatefully, angrily, or resentfully. Forgiveness is a movement of the heart.

- In your mind, picture him or her in front of you, hug them sending love to them from your heart. Do this until you feel a heartfelt connection with them. Can you love them no matter what?

- Can you hold them as a mother or father would hold their child, perhaps not agreeing, but still loving? Hold the person and feel the love dissolving the upset until it is gone.

Communicating with Others for Information

- Is there anyone who would give another viewpoint and not just side or commiserate with you?

- Is there someone from whom you can get more information about the person you are trying to forgive?

Perhaps you could talk with a brother or sister of the person, a friend, or others who might give you a better perspective of the person. For example, a client gained compassion and forgave his father after learning from his aunt how vicious his father's father had been to him.

Prayer

Prayer is a mighty vehicle for help in forgiveness. Say it over and over until a change is noticed. "I forgive you, you forgive me, we forgive each other." The key is to feel it happening each time.

All of the following types of sincere prayers are effective methods:

- Pray: For help to see it differently, like repeating over and over, "Please help me to see this in a different way."

- Pray: To be relieved of the upset altogether.

- Pray: For reconciliation if that is what you want.

Be prayed for by people. There are prayer groups in most churches that will pray for people. I have been prayed for and had significant results. I did not know at the time that I was being prayed for but learned about it later.

Recent research findings indicate that prayer positively affects healing. This has always been known in religious communities, and now scientific research in hospitals confirms it. People being prayed for recover sooner from serious problems—even when they do not know they are being prayed for. (Dossey 1993)

- Repeatedly say "I forgive" with full intention, thinking of all aspects of the situation. See in Chapter 4, *The Simplest Forgiveness Practice.*

Feelings

Communicating your feelings about a situation is essential. Without examining feelings, the upsets from a situation often will not release. You have to be aware of the upset to release it.

Write about or discuss with another person any of the feelings affecting you in a situation. They may be sadness, anger, hurt, depression, apathy, guilt, embarrassment, humiliation, regret, blame, or shame, to name a few. All the different feelings need to be addressed. You can ask:

- "How do I feel about what they did?"

- "What was I afraid of?

Journaling

Keep a log in your journal of:

- How often the upset comes into your mind during the day

- The situations that trigger it

- Earlier times this has occurred

- How forgiveness can change these recurrences

Appreciation

Any of these ways might be appropriate to give appreciation:

- Thank-you letter or flowers

- A letter of acknowledgment

- Acknowledging the person in person

Directly talk with your offender

If you can, it helps to let go of getting *your* point across. Just try to understand what *their* mindset was. You might be surprised.

- Can you do this without the dialogue becoming abusive or harmful to either of you?

Perspective: Different Ways of Seeing the Situation

Maintaining a rigid perspective or viewpoint keeps resentments and grudges in place and can impede or prevent forgiveness. Anything you do to modify that perspective will begin to alleviate its adverse effects. These methods can help you see the situation differently:

Projection
Turn around the situation you are evaluating and ask:
- Is this the same or similar in any way to something I have done to another or myself?

- Is this similar to a family pattern or the actions of someone else in my family?

Walking in the other's shoes
If you cannot answer these questions, then you need to learn a lot about this person to understand why they did what they did.
- How do they see the world? What do they fear? Love?

- What are their likes and dislikes?

- What was it like growing up in their family?

- What was it like being in their culture or time?

- What is their emotional intelligence?

- What was their expectation of you, of others?

Finding who
Often in our mind, there is a person or several people representing and often causing the broader situations in the world that upset you, for example, problems at an organization, government or even racism.
- Who are the people you think of when you see this upsetting situation?

- What is it about their behavior that upsets you?

- What does their face look like?

- What did they specifically do?

- Was every person like them doing the same thing?

- In your experience, have all of them been the same way?

Challenge
- Can you see your upset as a challenge to overcome rather than a punishment or attack? What would be the solution to this challenge?

- How would an impartial observer view this?

- Is there anything else going on here that you have a hunch about?

The Big Picture
- Are you sure they are not in your life to show you something about it?

- Could this be part of a Divine Plan or Karma? Or to show you a better, more effective, or happier way of being?

Turn it around
- Write down all the ways that they are correct and justified from their perspective.

Highest perspective – *See* the love
- What would the most loving part of yourself do? Why?

- How would you see them with the eyes of love? (For Christians, it could also be, what would Jesus do?)

Responsibility

Regardless of what a person says or does to you, your response is your responsibility, not anyone else's. Here are methods to help:

Validity and reality of rules broken
- List all of your values, laws, rules, or moral codes that they broke.

- Looking at each, ask: 1) Where did this rule come from? 2) Is it a valid rule, code, etc., or one that needs re-evaluation?

- Then ask 1) Do I have an unrealistic expectation of them to hold that law, value, or rule, especially if I have done the same thing in any way to others or myself? 2(Do I have an unrealistic expectation for myself to observe that law, value, or rule?

Amends and asking for forgiveness from another

- Do you need to make amends for the harm you have caused?

- What do you need to do to make it right?

Payoff

- What do you get by keeping the upset going? Write down any benefits. Who benefits and how?

- Is being right more important than being happy?

Being a Victim

- How long has your victimization by them been going on?How long is it okay to let them be in control of your happiness?

- Can you perceive yourself as a possible contributor to the problem and not just the victim?

Negative consequences of holding on to this upset

Sometimes people do not realize the negative effect that holding onto their unforgiven situation causes in their lives. Here are some questions to investigate this:

- List the negatives coming from this upset.

- What is happening to your family by holding onto it?

- How strong are love, peace, and joy in your life? Could resolving this situation increase love, peace, and joy in your life?

Personal Responsibility

- Do you want to keep this situation alive?

- Even if "they" seem to be the sole cause of the problem, how might be you be keeping it going?

- Is your logic getting in the way of the right thing to do in this situation?

- Are your emotions getting in the way of the right thing to do in this situation?

- Are you pressuring people to side with me to justify my position?

- What was your part in all of this? Did you make it worse?

- How can you take care of yourself better?

Thankfulness / Gratitude

In forgiveness work, looking for and acknowledging ways that the person has helped you is powerful. There are different possibilities and perspectives in every situation. Even as a negative role model, a person could have taught you something positive. When you extend thanks to them, you are sending love, the greatest healer.

- What can you be grateful for in this situation? What did you learn from them?

- How did they help you?

- How have they helped others?

- How did they affect a positive change in your life? Did their influence in your life make you stronger, more capable, or successful?

Having thankfulness in general in a person's life makes it easier. A great meditation/contemplation is to ask yourself, "What am I thankful for?" You ask this repeatedly until you are feeling more at peace and heartful toward them. I have seen people start this method, searching their minds deeply for something they were thankful for. In the end, they realize that they were grateful for many things in their life due to the person.

Notes

ENDNOTES

The Beginning
1. Cambridge University Press (2020
2. Pert (1999)

Chapter 1
1. Britannica (2019)
2. Fonseca, (2019)
3. Dubuc. B. et al. aep(2013)
4. Enright (1996)
5. Murphy, J. G.(1998)
6. Legaree (2007)
7. Shukla, S. 2019)
8. Worthington (2005)
9. Luskin (2000)
10. Enright et al., (2000)
11. Luskin (2000)
12. Enright, et. al, (1996)
13. Pandey (2020)
14. Rangganadhan & Todorov (2010).

Chapter 2
1. McCullough, M.E. (2008)
2. Carlsmith, et al. (2008)
3. Enright & Coyle (1998)
3a. McCullough, M.E. (2008)
4. Cambridge University Press (2020)
5. Corte, (1999)
6. McCullough, et al. (2000)
7. Hood(2009)
7a. Milam (2017)
8- 9. Gregoire, C. (2016)
10. Patterson (2011)
11. Eurich, (2017)
12. Worthington (2013)

Chapter3
1. Pronk (2010)

2.Merriam-Webster's learnersdictionary.com:
3. Cherry (2020)
4. Worthington,E.L. (2013)
5. Doorn, N., (2009)
6. McCullough 2013)
7. Maitrī (2021)
8. Chesed (2021)
9. Wilson, A. (2014)
10. Kok, B. E. et al. (2013)

Chapter 4
1. Reid (2000)
2. Worthington (2013)
3. Cialdina 2006
4. Worthington ,E.L. (2013)
5. Ackerman, C.E. (2020)
6- 7. Souders, B, (2020)
8. Oosterwijk, et al. (2012)
9. White, C.C. (2017)
10. APA (2005)
11. Eskelinen & Ollonena (2011)
12. Emmons (2003)
13- 14. Walia, A (2019)

Chapter 5
1 NSCDC 2010
2 Seligman (2004)
3 Emmons, R. A.,(2003)
4 -5. Walia (2019)
6. Samples, B (1993)
7. Your Dictionary
8. QBI (2019)
9 Dubuc, B. (2015)
10 - 11. Lynch (2007)
12. McCullough (1997)
13. Widstrom et al(2019)
14. Engel (2001)
Chapter 6
1. Ebersöhn (2012).
2. Low (2020)
3. Worthington & Scherer,(2004)
4. Worthington, E.L. (2013)
5. Pant, A. (2019)

6. Varvogli, L. (2018)
7. Toussaint (2016)
8. Worthington (2004)
9. Witvliet et al. .2001)
10. Benson (1976)
10a. Carnes (1997)
11. Better Babies (2019)
12. McCullough (2008)
13- 14. Fessler, L. (2018)

Chapter 7
1- 2. Ayan, S. (2018)
3. Hanson, 2020)
3a. Hanson (2013)
4. Better Brains for Babies (2019)
Table of contents
5. Dubuc (2015)
5a. QBI 2019
6- 6a. Lewis P37
7. Amen, D.G. (2006)a and b
8. Dubuc, B. (2012) -THE
AMYGDALA intermediate
9. McCullough (2008)
10. Science Daily (2020)
11. Do Amaral & de Oliviera (2003)
12. Frantz (2005)
13. PreFrontal cortex, (2020)
14. Amen, D.G. (2006)a
15. McCullough (2008)
15a. NCLD (2008)
15b. Pre-Frontal cortex, (2020)
15c. Amen, D.G. (2006)a.
16. Arnsten, et al. (2012)
17- 17a. Dubuc, B.-iep (2013)
17b. Lewis et al. (2000)
17c. Dubuc, B.-iep (2013)
17d. Dubuc, B. -aep (2013)
18a. Geary (2011)
18b. Tau & Peterson (2010)
18c. Dubuc. B. et al. aep(2013)
19. Maclean (1990)
20. Prettyman (1997)
21. Dubuc. B. et al. aep(2013)
21a. Mattmiller, B. (1998)

22. Maclean (1990)
23. Van der Denne (2005)
24. Hobson (2017)
25. Do Amaral & de Oliviera (2003)
26. Gino & Norton (2013)
27. Prettyman (1997)
28. Graybiel (2008)
29- 30. Maclean (1990)
31. Bernstein, R.(2016)
32. Fear (2020)
33.Sympathetic nervous system(2020)
34. Elsevier (2016)
35. Schaarschmidt (2018)
36.Oregon Public Broadcasting (2020)
37. Neuron (2019)
37a. QBI (2019)
37b. Greene, A. (2010)
37c. Cherry (2020)
38. Gregoire, C. (2016)
39. Bergland, C (2014)
40. Van der Kolk, B. A. (2014).
41. Witvliet, et al. (2015)
42. Minamoto & Haruno (2016)
43 -44. Linden (2007)
45. Clever Bytes Ltd.,(2020)
46. Shen (2018)
47. Wade, et al. (2002)
48. Garry & Wade (2005)
49. Hogenboom (2013)
50. French (2015)
51. Brainerd & Reyna (2005)
52. Linden, (2007)

Chapter 8
1. Moccia, et al.(2018)
2. Capri 1996
3. Prevent Child Abuse America (2016)
4. Frontiers. (2017)
4a. HealthDirect (2019)
5. Prevent Child Abuse America (2016)

6. Elsevier (20016)
7. Prevent Child Abuse America (2016)
8. 9. Baggaley, K.(2016)
10. Davis, T. (2018)
11- 13. McKay, et al. (1981)
14. Davis, T. (2018)
15- 16. Resilience- psych today (2019)
17. Hendriksen, E. (2017)
18. Resilience- psych today 2019.
19. Coping skills for kids (2019)
20- 23. Varvogli, L. (2018)

Chapter 9
1. Luskin (2000)
2. Shetgiri R. (2013)
3. McCullough 2008
4. Exline (2013)
5. Dugatkin 2005
6. McCullough 2008
7. Carlsmith, et al. (2008)
8. Jaffee (2011
9. McCullough (2008)
10. Jaffee (2011)
11. Oneri Uzun (2018)
12. McCullough (2008)
13. Hanson (2014)
14. Lucus, et al. (2010)
15.-16. Lewis, et al. 2000
17. Groupo Mcontigo (2018)
18. Weir (2014))

Chapter 10
1. Barcaccia, et al. (2020)
2 - 3. Blakeslee (2005)
4. Figley (2000)
5. Hossack & Bentall (1996)
6. Koziey & McLeod (1987)
7. Blakeslee (2005)
8. Da Silva & Witvliet, (2016)
9. Marcoux (2015)
10. Oman, et al. (2008)

Chapter 11
1-3. Shetgiri R. (2013)
4. American Osteopathic Association (2017)
5. Shetgiri R. (2013)
6. Hinduja & Patchin (2014)
7. Scheff, S. (2019)
8. Baggaley, K.(2016)
9-10. Shetgiri R. (2013)
11. Cherry (2020),
12. Dubuc (2015)
13. Greene, A. (2010)

Chapter 12
1- 1a. Carpi (1996)
2. Web MD Medical Reference (2019)
3. Brearley, B. (2019)
4. Vazqeuz (2016)
5. De Beauport (1996)
6. Psychology Today (2020)
7. Young 2004
8. Hendriksen, E. (2017)
9-10. Shetgiri (2013)
11 Figley (2002)
12 – 13. van der kolk 2009
14 Starnes (2005)
15. Arrien (1991)

Chapter 13
1. Foltz-Gray, (2002)

Chapter 14
1. Dugatkin (2005)
2. Taniguchi (1931)

REFERENCES

- Ackerman, C.E. (2020) What is Solution-Focused Therapy: 3 Essential Techniques, https://positivepsychology.com/solution-focused-therapy/ retrieved 8/21/2020
- Ahirwar, G., Tiwari, G. K., & Rai, P. K. (2019b). Are the Big Five Personality dimensions uniformly relevant to understand the forgiveness of children? IAHRW International Journal of Social Sciences Review, 7(5), 852-887.
- Ahirwara, G., Tiwari, G.K., Rai, P.K. (2019) Exploring the Nature, Attributes and Consequences of Forgiveness in Children, Psychological Thought, 2019, Vol. 12(2), 214–231, https://doi.org/10.5964/psyct.v12i2.347 retrieved 9/5/2020
- Alexander-Scott, N. (2015) Addressing Toxic Stress In Young Children In Rhode Island, https://health.ri.gov/publications/presentations/2015ToxicStress.pdf retrieved 10/7/2020
- Amen, D.G. (2006)a. Retrieved 6-4-06 from amenclinics.com/bp/systems/limbic
- Amen, D.G. (2006)b. Retrieved 6-4-06: amenclinics.com/bp/articles.php?articleID=10
- Armstrong, T., (2019) "Multiple Intelligences." http://www.institute4learning.com/resources/ articles/multiple-intelligences/ Retrieved 8/28/2019
- Arrien, A. (1991). Personal notes from lectures in 1991
- Arnsten, A., Mazure, C. M., & Sinha, R. (2012). This is your brain in meltdown. Scientific American, 306(4), 48–53. https://doi.org/10.1038/scientificamerican0412-48 retrieved 8/18/2020
- APA (2005) Controlling Anger — Before It Controls You. https://www.apa.org/topics/anger/control retrieved 8/16/2020
- Ayan, S. (2018) The Brain's Autopilot Mechanism Steers Consciousness https://www.scientificamerican.com/article/the-brains-autopilot-mechanism-steers-consciousness/ retrieved 10/20/2020
- Baggaley, K.(2016) How Being Bullied Affects Your Adulthood, https://getpocket.com/explore/item/how-being-bullied-affects-your-adulthood?utm_source=pocket-newtab retrieved 2/July 2020
- Barcaccia, B., Salvati, M., Pallini, S. et al. (2020) The bitter taste of revenge: Negative affect, depression and anxiety. Current Psychology. https://doi.org/10.1007/s12144-020-00643-1 retrieved 1/26/2021
- BBCAHT (2018)- Big Bend Coalition Against Human Trafficking -Building Awareness, Taking Action Power Point Presentation
- Benson, H. (1976). The Relaxation Response, NY: HarperTorch
- Bergland, C. (2014) Chronic Stress Can Damage Brain Structure and Connectivity https://www.psychologytoday.com/blog/the-athletes-

way/201402/chronic-stress-can-damage-brain-structure-and-connectivity?destination=blog/the-athletes-way/201402/chronic-stress-can-damage-brain-structure-and-connectivity downloaded 11/22/2014

- Bernstein, R.(2016) The Mind and Mental Health: How Stress Affects the Brain, https://www.tuw.edu/health/how-stress-affects-the-brain/ retrieved 10/13/2020

- Better Brains for Babies (2019) "Effects of Stress on Brain Development" https://www.bbbgeorgia.org/effects-of-stress retrieved 11/2/2019

- Brearley, B. (2019) "The Unintended Consequences of Leading By Fear" The Thoughtful Leader, https://www.thoughtfulleader.com/leading-by-fear/ Retrieved 8/28/2019

- Britannica, T. Editors of Encyclopaedia (2019, June 6). *Agape. Encyclopedia Britannica.* https://www.britannica.com/topic/agape retrieved 1/31/2021

- Cambridge University Press (2020) https://dictionary.cambridge.org/us/dictionary/english/subconscious Retrieved 10-12-2020

- Carlsmith, K. M., Wilson, T. D., & Gilbert, D. T. (2008). The paradoxical consequences of revenge. Journal of Personality and Social Psychology, 95, 1316–1324.

- Carnes, Ph.D., P. J. (1997). The Betrayal Bond: Breaking free of exploitive relationships. Florida: Health Communications, Inc.

- Carpi, J. (1996). Stress: It's Worse Than You Think, Psychology Today, Jan/Feb 96 Retrieved 4/23/2006 from psychologytoday.com/articles/pto-19960101-000027.html

- Cherry, K. (2020)Priming and the Psychology of Memory https://www.verywellmind.com/priming-and-the-psychology-of-memory-4173092 Retrieved 2/15/2021

- Chesed, (2021) https://en.wikipedia.org/wiki/Chesed retrieved 1/25/2021

- Cialdini, R.B., (2006) Influence: The Psychology of Persuasion, Revised Edition -Harper Business

- Coping skills for kids (2019)Deep Breathing exercises for children.https://copingskillsforkids.com/deep-breathing-exercises-for-kids retrieved 10/27/2020

- Cortes, A. de J. (1999). Antecedents to the conflict between religion and psychology in America. Journal of Psychology and Theology, retrieved 10/15/2020

- Coyle, C. T., & Enright, R. D. (1998). Forgiveness education with adult learners. In T. Pourchot, & M. C. Smith (Eds.), Adult learning and development: Perspectives from educational psychology. Mahawah, NJ: L. Erivaum.

- CTDC (2008) Family Members Are Involved Are In Nearly Half Of Child Trafficking Cases, Counter-Trafficking Data Collaborative https://www.iom.int/sites/default/files/our_work/DMM/MAD/Counter-trafficking%20Data%20Brief%20081217.pdf retrieved 11/4/2020

- da Silva, Sérgio & Witvliet, Charlotte & Riek, Blake. (2016). Self-forgiveness and forgiveness-seeking in response to rumination: Cardiac and emotional responses of transgressors. The Journal of Positive Psychology. 1-11. 10.1080/17439760.2016.1187200.

- Davis, T., (2018) Resilience 101: How to Be a More Resilient Person, https://www.psychologytoday.com/us/blog/click-here-happiness/201803/resilience-101-how-be-more-resilient-person retrieved 10/5/2020\

- De Beauport, E. (1996) "Crossing the Threshold of the Unconscious: Into The Basic Brain," Retrieved 7-13-06 from www.motley-focus.com/crossing.html Taken from her book: *The Three Faces of the Mind: Developing Your Mental, Emotional, and Behavioral Intelligences*. Elaine de Beauport with Aura Sofia Diaz. Quest Books. (1996) Wheaton: The Theosophical Publishing House.

- Do Amaral, J.& de Oliveira, J. (2003). Limbic System: The Center of Emotions, Retrieved 7-12-2006 from http://www.healing-arts.org/n-r-limbic.htm

- Doorn, N., (2009) The Place of Forgiveness in Transitional Justice Practices, In S. Bloch-Schulman, & D. White (Eds.), (2009) Forgiveness: Probing the Boundaries (pp. 191-209). Inter-discplinary Press. Retrieved 5/30/2020

- DoSomething (2020) 11 FACTS ABOUT HUMAN TRAFFICKING https://www.dosomething.org/us/facts/11-facts-about-human-trafficking retrieved 11/2/2020

- Dossey, L. (1993). *Healing Words- The Power of Prayer and the Practice of Medicine*, NY: Harper Collins

- Dubuc, B. (2002). "The Evolutionary Layers Of The Human Brain," *The Brain from Top to Bottom* https://thebrain.mcgill.ca/flash/i/i_05/i_05_cr/i_05_cr_her/i_05_cr_her.html Retrieved 8/28/19

- Dubuc, B. 2012) THE AMYGDALA AND ITS ALLIES- Intermediate, *The Brain from Top to Bottom* https://thebrain.mcgill.ca/flash/i/i_04/i_04_cr/i_04_cr_peu/i_04_cr_peu.html retrieved 10/20/2020

- Dubuc. B. et al. aep(2013) Advanced Evolutionary Psychology, *The Brain from Top to Bottom* http://thebrain.mcgill.ca/flash/a/a_05/a_05_p/a_05_p_her/a_05_p_her.html retrieved 10/13/2020

- Dubuc, B.-iep (2013) Intermediate Evoloutionary pscyhology, *The Brain from Top to Bottom* http://thebrain.mcgill.ca/flash/i/i_05/i_05_p/i_05_p_her/i_05_p_her.html retrieved 10/13/2020

- Dubuc, B.(2015) Plasticity In Neural Networks, *The Brain from Top to Bottom*, https://thebrain.mcgill.ca/flash/d/d_07/d_07_cl/d_07_cl_tra/d_07_cl_tra.html Retrieved 2/15/2021

- Dugatkin, L. (2005) Why don't we just kiss and make up? *New Scientist*, 5/7/05
- Ebersöhn, Liesel. (2012). Adding 'Flock' to 'Fight and Flight': A Honeycomb of Resilience Where Supply of Relationships Meets Demand for Support. Journal of Psychology in Africa. 22. 29-42. 10.1080/14330237.2012.10874518. retrieved 10/21/2020
- Elsevier (2016) Changes in brain networks may help youth adapt to childhood adversity, https://medicalxpress.com/news/2016-07-brain-networks-youth-childhood-adversity.html retrieved 1/10/2020
- Emmons, R. A., & McCullough, M. E. (2003). Counting blessings versus burdens: An experimental investigation of gratitude and subjective well-being in daily life. Journal of Personality & Social Psychology, 88, 377-389. Retrieved 2/22/2017
- Engel, B. (2001) The Power of Apology: Healing Steps to Transform All Your Relationships, NY: John Wiley & Sons, Inc
- Enright, R. D., Freedman, S., & Rique, J. (1998). "The psychology of interpersonal forgiveness." In R. D. Enright & J. North (Eds.), Exploring Forgiveness (pp. 46–62). University of Wisconsin Press
- Enright, R.D., and the Human Development Study Group (1996). "Counseling within the forgiveness triad" Counseling and Values, (40)
- Enright, R. D., Coyle, C. T. (1998) Researching the Process Model of Forgiveness Within Psychological Interventions , In Dimensions of Forgiveness: Psychological Research & Theological Perspectives, Everett L. Worthington (Editor) Templeton Foundation Press (1998)
- Enright, R.D., Fitzgibbons, R.P. (2000). Helping Clients Forgive: An Empirical Guide For Resolving Anger And Restoring Hope, Washington DC: American Psychological Assoc.
- Eskelinen, M, Ollonena, P, (2011) "Measurement of Pessimism: Hopelessness Scale", Anticancer Research, November 2011 vol. 31 no. 11 4019-4023
- Exline, J.J.,The Thorny Issue of Forgiveness: A Psychological Perspective, (2013) 13 Pepp. Disp. Resol. L.J. Iss. 1 http://digitalcommons.pepperdine.edu/drlj/vol13/iss1/2 retrieved 12/9/2015 In the Pepperdine Dispute Resolution Law Journal, Vol. 13, Iss. 1 [2013], Art. 2
- Eurich, T. (2017) "The Right Way To Be Introspective." https://ideas.ted.com/the-right-way-to-be-introspective-yes-theres-a-wrong-way/ retrieved 7/28/2019
- Fear (2019) https://en.wikipedia.org/wiki/Fear Retrieved 1 June 2019
- Fessler, L. (2018) Who Should You Trust? Psychologists Have a Surprising Answer, https://getpocket.com/explore/item/who-should-you-trust-psychologists-have-a-surprising-answer?utm_source=pocket-newtab retrieved 6/7/2020
- Figley, C. R. (2000). "Post-Traumatic Stress Disorder," American Association for Marriage and Family Therapy -AAMFT -Clinical Update Volume 2, Issue

5, Sept. 2000, Retrieved 12/29/05
www.aamft.org/families/Consumer_Updates /PTSD_AAMFT
_Clinical_Update.htm

- Figley, C. R. (2002). "AAMFT Consumer Update on Post-Traumatic Stress Disorder," American Association for Marriage and Family Therapy, Retrieved 5/15/06 www.aamft.org/families/Consumer_Updates/PTSD.asp

- Finklea, K., Fernandes-Alcantara, A.L., Siskin, A.(2015) Sex Trafficking of Children in the United States: Overview and Issues for Congress, Congressional Research Service, https://fas.org/sgp/crs/misc/R41878.pdf retrieved 11/4/2020

- Foltz-Gray, D., (2002) *Start Forgiving*, Arthritis Today, 9-10/2002. http://www.drrandijones.com/newsltr4.htm retrieved 2003

- Fonseca, C. (2019) Your Brain Is a Liar: 7 Common Cons Your Brain Uses, https://www.psychologytoday.com/us/blog/parenting-new-generation/201905/your-brain-is-liar-7-common-cons-your-brain-uses retrieved 7/24/2020

- Frantz, R. (2005). "Introduction to Intuition," Two Minds: Intuition and Analysis in the History of Economic Thought, Springer. Retrieved 5-03-07 from http://www-rohan.sdsu.edu/~frantz/docs/Chapter1.pdf

- Frontiers. (2017). How self-regulation can help young people overcome setbacks. www.sciencedaily.com/releases/2017/05/170529101502.htm Retrieved May 29, 2020

- Giedd J. N. (2020). Adolescent brain and the natural allure of digital media. Dialogues in clinical neuroscience, 22(2), 127–133. https://doi.org/10.31887/DCNS.2020.22.2/jgiedd)

- Gino, F., Norton, M.I.,(2013) Why Rituals Work, https://www.scientificamerican.com/article/why-rituals-work/ retrieved 10/20/2020

- Greene, A. (2010). Making Connections. *Scientific American Mind,* 21(3), 22-29. Retrieved February 15, 2021, from http://www.jstor.org/stable/24943081

- Gregoire, C. (2016) How To Wire Your Brain For Happiness, https://www.huffpost.com/entry/how-tiny-joyful-moments-c_n_4108363 retrieved 10/13/2020

- Grupo MContigo (2018)When a Parent Has Paranoid Personality Disorder, https://exploringyourmind.com/parent-paranoid-personality-disorder/ retrieved 11/17/2020

- Hanson, R., (2013) Hardwiring Happiness: The New Brain Science of Contentment, Calm, and Confidence. Harmony Books (Random House)

- Hanson, R. (2020) Take in the Good, https://www.rickhanson.net/take-in-the-good/ Retrieved 11/11/2020

- Harvard University -Center on the Developing Child (2007). A Science-Based Framework for Early Childhood Policy: Using Evidence to Improve

Outcomes in Learning, Behavior, and Health for Vulnerable Children. http://www.developingchild.harvard.edu retrieved 3/28/2020

- Harvard University- The Center on the Developing Child (2020)Toxic Stress Derails Healthy Development, https://developingchild.harvard.edu/resources/toxic-stress-derails-healthy-development/ retrieved 2/23/2020

- HealthDirect (2019) Building Resilience, https://www.healthdirect.gov.au/resilience retrieved 1/26/2021

- Hendriksen, E., (2017) 6 Ways to Build Your Resilience https://www.quickanddirtytips.com/health-fitness/mental-health/6-ways-to-build-your-resilience retrieved 10-5/2020

- Hinduja, S. & Patchin, J. W. (2019). Cyberbullying fact sheet: Identification, Prevention, and Response. Cyberbullying Research Center. Retrieved [insert date], from https://cyberbullying.org/Cyberbullying-Identification-Prevention-Response-2019.pdf.

- Ho'oponopono (1999) From classes with: Keoki Sousa, Sept-Oct 1999, Maui Community College, Maui, HI and Kapi'ioho Lyons Naone, June 1999, Bailey House, Maui, HI

- Ho'oponopono - 2019 retrieved 8/7/2019, from https://en.wikipedia.org/ wiki/ Ho'oponopono

- Hood, R.W., Hill, P.C., Spilka, C.B. (2009) The Psychology of Religion 4th Edition. https://dl.uswr.ac.ir/bitstream/Hannan/130506/1/Ralph_W._Hood__Jr.%2 C_Peter_C._Hill_PhD%2C_Bernard_Spilka_The_Psychology_of_Religion% 2C_Fourth_Edition_An_Empirical_Appr-4ZP-JF3S.pdf retrieved 10/15/2020

- Hossack, A., Bentall, R.P. (1996) Elimination of posttraumatic symptomatology by relaxation and visual-kinesthetic dissociation. J Trauma Stress 9, 99–110. https://doi.org/10.1007/BF02116836 retrieved 10/30/2020

- Ikiz, F. E., Mete-Otlu, B., Asıcı, E. (2015). Beliefs of Counselor Trainees about Forgiveness. Educational Sciences: Theory & Practice. 15. 10.12738/estp.2015.2.2205. retrieved Feb 10, 2020

- Interpol (2020) Human trafficking https://www.interpol.int/en/Crimes/Human-trafficking retrieved 11/3/2020

- Jaffe, E., (2011)"The Complicated Psychology of Revenge" Observer Vol.24, No.8 October 2011 https://www.psychologicalscience.org/index.php/publications/observer/201 1/october11

- Kok, B. E., Coffey, K. A., Cohn, M. A., Catalino, L. I., Vacharkulksemsuk, T., Algoe, S. B., Brantley, M., & Fredrickson, B. L. (2013). How positive emotions build physical health: perceived positive social connections account for the upward spiral between positive emotions and vagal tone. *Psychological*

science, 24(7), 1123–1132. https://doi.org/10.1177/0956797612470827
retrieved 2/2/2021

- Koziey, P. W., & McLeod, G. L. (1987). Visual-kinesthetic dissociation in treatment of victims of rape. Professional Psychology: Research and Practice, 18(3), 276–282. https://doi.org/10.1037/0735-7028.18.3.276 retrieved 10/30/2020

- Legaree, T., Turner, J., Lollis, S. (2007) "Forgiveness and Therapy: A Critical Review of Conceptualizations, Practices, and Values Found In the Literature." Journal of Marital and Family Therapy. The American Association for Marriage & Family Therapy. Retrieved 2/02/09 from: www.highbeam.com/doc/1P3-1270855471.html

- Lenroot, R. K., & Giedd, J. N. (2006). Brain development in children and adolescents: insights from anatomical magnetic resonance imaging. Neuroscience and biobehavioral reviews, 30(6), 718–729. https://doi.org/10.1016/j.neubiorev.2006.06.001)

- Lewis, T., Amini, & Landon, (2000).A General Theory of Love, NY: Random House.

- Linden, D., (2007) The Accidental Mind, Belknap Press

- Low, P (2020) Overview of the Autonomic Nervous System. https://www.merckmanuals.com/home/brain,-spinal-cord,-and-nerve-disorders/autonomic-nervous-system-disorders/overview-of-the-autonomic-nervous-system# retrieved 2/2/2021

- Lucas, T., Young, J. D., Zhdanova, L., & Alexander, S. (2010). Self and other justice beliefs, impulsivity, rumination, and forgiveness: Justice beliefs can both prevent and promote forgiveness. Personality and Individual Differences, 49, 851–856 retrieved 11/2/2020

- Luethi, M., Meier, B., & Sandi, C. (2009). Stress effects on working memory, explicit memory, and implicit memory for neutral and emotional stimuli in healthy men. Frontiers in Behavioral Neuroscience, 1-9. retrieved 8/17/2020

- Luskin, F. (2000). Forgive for Good: A Proven Prescription for Health and Happiness, pp 77-93, San Francisco: Harper.

- Luskin, F. (2007) Forgive for Love: The Missing Ingredient for a Healthy and Lasting Relationship, NY: Harper One.

- Lynch, M.J. (2007) Big Prisons, Big Dreams: Crime and the Failure of America's Penal System, Rutgers University Press.

- MacLean, P. D. (1990). *The Triune Brain in Evolution*, NY: Plenum

- Marcoux, E.(2016) Meditation and Neuroscience, https://cornerstonemindfulness.com/research-post/ retrieved 9/27/2016

- Mattmiller, B. (1998) Professor finds that in shirts, as well as skin, color matters. https://news.wisc.edu/professor-finds-that-in-shirts-as-well-as-skin-color-matters/retrieved 10/20/2020

- McCullough ME, Sandage SJ, Worthington EL Jr. (1997) To forgive is human: How to put your past in the past. Downers Grove, IL: InterVarsity Press.
- McCullough, M., Worthington, E., Rachal, C. (1997). Interpersonal Forgiving in Close Relationships. Journal of personality and social psychology. 73. 321-36. 10.1037/0022-3514.73.2.321. retrieved 9/12/2020
- McCullough, M. E., Pargament, K. I., & Thoresen, C. E. (2000). The psychology of forgiveness: History, conceptual issues, and overview. In M. E. McCullough, K. I. Pargament, & C. E. Thoresen (Eds.), Forgiveness: Theory, research, and practice (pp. 1-14). New York: Guildford Press.(2001)
- McCullough, M.E. (2008). Beyond Revenge: The evolution of the forgiveness instinct. Jossey-Bass.
- McCullough, M. E., Kurzban, R., & Tabak, B. A. (2013). Cognitive systems for revenge and forgiveness. *The Behavioral and brain sciences, 36*(1), 1–15. https://doi.org/10.1017/S0140525X11002160 retrieved 8/4/2020
- McKay, M., Davis, M., & Fanning, P. (1981). Thoughts & Feelings: The Art of Cognitive Stress Intervention, Oakland: New Harbinger.
- Merriam-Webster (2019), learnersdictionary.com/definition/accept, Retrieved 2June2016.
- Milam, M., Borrello, N., & Pooler, J. (2017). The Survivor Centered, Trauma-Informed Approach. The United States Attorney Bulletin 65, p39-43.
- Minamoto, T., Haruno, M.(2016) Higher revenge rumination trait prevents retrieval of positive memory toward a transgressor: A study with an association memory task. A presentation at the 31st International Congress of Psychology, Yokohama Japan, retrieved 7/25/2016
- Moccia, L., Mazza, M., Di Nicola, M., & Janiri, L. (2018). The Experience of Pleasure: A Perspective Between Neuroscience and Psychoanalysis. Frontiers in human neuroscience, 12, 359. https://doi.org/10.3389/fnhum.2018.00359 retrieved 1/31/2021
- Murphy, J. G.(1998) Forgiveness and mercy,DOI: 10.4324/9780415249126-K024-1 version: v1, Published online: 1998 Retrieved December 22, 2019, from https://www.rep.routledge.com/articles/thematic forgiveness-and-mercy/v-1
- NCLD -National Center for Learning Disabilities, Inc. (2008), Executive Function Fact Sheet, http://www.ldonline.org/article/24880) Retrieved 5/4/2019
- Neuron- 2019 Retrieved 1 Jun 2019 https://en.wikipedia.org/wiki/Neuron
- NSCDC - National Scientific Council on the Developing Child (2010). Early Experiences Can Alter Gene Expression and Affect Long-Term Development, Retrieved 7/7/2019 from www.developingchild.harvard.edu.
- Oman, D., Shapiro, S. L., Thoresen, C. E., Plante, T. G., & Flinders, T. (2008). Meditation lowers stress and supports forgiveness among college students: a randomized controlled trial. Journal of American college health : J

of ACH, 56(5), 569–578. https://doi.org/10.3200/JACH.56.5.569-578 retrieved 7/7/2020

- Oneri Uzun, Gizem. (2018). Examining The Relations Between Revenge, Forgiveness And Guilt Levels Of High School Students. IIOAB Journal. 9. 89-100. retrieved 10/12/2020
- Oosterwijk, S., Lindquist, K. A., Anderson, E., Dautoff, R., Moriguchi, Y., & Barrett, L. F. (2012). States of mind: emotions, body feelings, and thoughts share distributed neural networks. NeuroImage, 62(3), 2110–2128. https://doi.org/10.1016/j. neuroimage.2012.05.079 retrieved 5.28.2020
- Oregon Public Broadcasting (2020) Hacking Your Mind - Us vs. Them video PBS aired 09/23/2020 Made possible by a major grant from the the National Science Foundation. 9/23/2020
- Pandey, R., Tiwari, G. K., Pandey, R., Mandal, S. P., Mudgal, S., Parihar, P., Rai, P. K., Tiwari, A. S., Shukla, M. (2020). The relationship between self-esteem and self-forgiveness: Understanding the mediating role of positive and negative self-compassion [Preprint]. Preprints. https://doi.org/10.22541/au.158981530.01103201 retrieved 9/21/2020
- Pant, A. (2019) The Role of Wind in a Tree's Life http://awesci.com/the-role-of-wind-in-a-trees-life/ retrieved 10/28/20
- Patterson, K., Grenny, J., McMillan, R., Switzler, A., (2011) Crucial Conversations: Tools for Talking When Stakes Are High, Second Edition, McGraw-Hill Education
- Pert C.B.,(1999), Molecules of Emotion: The Science Behind Mind-Body Medicine, Simon & Schuster
- PreFrontal cortex, (2020) https://en.wikipedia.org/wiki/Prefrontal_cortex retrieved 10/13/2020
- Prettyman, J.W. (1997). *Deep And Deeper: Deep Blue vs. The Triune Brain,* www.americanreview.us/deepblue.htm Retrieved 7-12-06
- Prevent Child Abuse America (2016) The Facilitator's Guide to Resilience - A discussion guide to accompany screenings of the documentary film http://preventchildabuse.org/wp-content/uploads/2016/09/Resilience-Guide-FINAL.pdf retrieved 2/18/2020
- Pronk, T. M., Karremans, J. C., Overbeek, G., Vermulst, A. A., & Wigboldus, D. H. J. (2010). What it takes to forgive: When and why executive functioning facilitates forgiveness. *Journal of Personality and Social Psychology, 98*(1), 119-131. https://doi.org/10.1037/a0017875 retrieved 7/8/2020
- Psychology Today (2019) "Emotional Intelligence," https://www.psychologytoday.com/us/ basics/emotional intelligence Retrieved 8/28/2019
- Psychology Today (2019) Resilience, https://www.psychologytoday. com/us/basics/resilience retrieved 9-29-2020
- QBI - Queensland Brain Institute (2018)The Brain-Learning and Memory, Issue two. www.qbi.uq.edu.au/learning Retrieved 2/15/2021

- QBI - Queensland Brain Institute (2019) What makes memories stronger? https://qbi.uq.edu.au/brain-basics/memory/what-makes-memories-stronger Retrieved 2/15/2021

- Rangganadhan, A. R., & Todorov, N. (2010). Personality and self-forgiveness: The roles of shame, guilt, empathy and conciliatory behavior. Journal of Social and Clinical Psychology, 29(1), 1–22. https://doi.org/10.1521/jscp.2010.29.1.1 retrieved 1/30/21

- Reid, F., Hoffmann, D. (2000). *Long Night's Journey Into Day: South Africa's Search for Truth & Reconciliation*, Iris Films, Retrieved 2/25/2008 from www.irisfilms.org/longnight/

- Schaarschmidt , T. (2018) The Art of Lying, https://www.scientificamerican.com/article/the-art-of-lying/?print=true retrieved 7/24/2020

- Scheff, S. (2019) Adult Cyberbullying Is More Common Than You Think New study: How online hate is impacting all ages and ways we can turn it around. https://www.psychologytoday.com/gb/blog/ shame-nation/201911/adult-cyberbullying-is-more-common-you-think retrieved 1/3/2021

- Samples, B (1993) The Metaphoric Mind: A Celebration of Creative Consciousness, Jalmar Pr; second edition

- Seligman, M. E. (2004). "Happiness Interventions That Work," Authentic Happiness Coaching News, Vol 2, No. 10 5/3/2004, Retrieved 7/13/2004 from: AuthenticHappinessCoaching.com

- Shehan, S., Aufmuth, A. (2017)Domestic Child Sex Trafficking and Children Missing from Care, United States Attorneys' Bulletin November 2017, Volume 65, Number 6, retrieved 11/3/2020

- Shetgiri R. (2013). Bullying and victimization among children. Advances in pediatrics, 60(1), 33–51. doi:10.1016/j.yapd.2013.04.004 retrieved 11/23/2019

- Shukla, S., Tiwari, G.K., & Pramod Kumar Rai, P.K. (2019) Positive Psychology and Development of Children: A Paradigm Shift, Conference Paper- : Life-Span Human Development. https://www.researchgate.net/publication/335757838 retrieved 9-4-2020

- Souders, B, (2020) Classic Therapy Questions Therapists Tend To Ask, https://positivepsychology.com/common-therapy-questions/ retrieved 4/14/20230

- Starnes, G. (2005) "The Psychophysiology of Trauma" Returning Warriors Blog, 5/16/05 Retrieved 1-17-09 www.returningwarriors.org/2005_05_01_archive.html

- Steiner, C. *Transactional Analysis, and the Triune Brain* Retrieved 7-9-06 from http://www.emotional-literacy.com/triune.htm

- Taniguchi, M. (1931). *Holy Sutra*, Special Maui Edition 1987 Hawaii: Seicho-No-Ie.

- Toussaint, L. L., Shields, G. S., & Slavich, G. M. (2016). Forgiveness, Stress, and Health: a 5-Week Dynamic Parallel Process Study. Annals of behavioral medicine: a publication of the Society of Behavioral Medicine, 50(5), 727–735. https://doi.org/10.1007/s12160-016-9796-6 retrieved 10-7-2020

- Toussaint, L., Williams, D., Musick, & Everson-Rose, (2008). "Why forgiveness may protect against depression" Personality and Mental Health, 2, 89-103.

- Toussaint, Loren & D Owen, Amy & Cheadle, Alyssa. (2011). "Forgive to Live: Forgiveness, Health, and Longevity," Journal of Behavioral Medicine. 35. 375-86. 10.1007/s10865-011-9362-4.

- Towey, S. (2013) "Impact of Fear and Anxiety", Taking charge of your health and wellbeing, https://www.takingcharge.csh.umn.edu/impact-fear-and-anxiety, Retrieved 8/11/2019

- Ulrich, M.W. (2020) Know the three types of stress that can affect children https://www.floridatoday.com/story/life/wellness/2020/06/ 02/know-three-types-stress-can-affect-children/5278460002/ retrieved 10-7-2020

- Van der Dennen, J.M.G. (2005). "Ritualized 'Primitive' Warfare And Rituals In War: Phenocopy, Homology, Or..?" Retrieved 6-12-06: WWW.irs.ub.rug.nl/ppn/280499396

- Van der Kolk, B. A. (2014). The Body Keeps The Score: Brain, Mind, And Body In The Healing Of Trauma. New York: Viking.

- Van der Kolk, B., (2009) "Specialized Treatment Approaches" The Trauma Center at Justice Resource Institute, retrieved 1/21/09 www.traumacenter.org/clients/spec_svcs_treatment.php

- Varvogli, L. (2018) The Best Relaxation Techniques for Children, https://varvogli.com/2018/02/23/the-best-relaxation-techniques-for-children/ retrieved10/27/2020

- Vazquez, L.(2016)What Fear does to your brain, https://bigthink.com/laurie-vazquez/what-fear-does-to-your-brain-and-how-to-stop-it, retrieved 8/11/2019

- Walia, A (2019) "How Gratitude Literally Alters The Human Heart & Molecular Structure Of The Brain" Retrieved 10/25/2019 from https://www.collective-evolution.com, Published February 14, 2019

- Web MD Medical Reference (2019) "What are the consequences of long-term stress?" https://www.webmd.com/balance/stress-management/qa/what-are-the-consequences-of-longterm-stress Retrieved 11/2/2019

- Weir, K., (2014) The Lasting Impact of Neglect, https://www.apa.org/monitor/2014/06/neglect retrieved 11/10/2020

- White, C.C. (2017) Putting resilience and resilience surveys under the microscope, https://acestoohigh.com/2017/02/05/ retrieved 4/5/2020

- Widström, AM, Brimdyr, K, Svensson, K, Cadwell, K, Nissen, E (2019) Skin-to-skin contact the first hour after birth, underlying implications and clinical practice. Acta Paediatr. 2019 Jul;108(7):1192-1204. doi: 10.1111/apa.14754. Epub 2019 Mar 13.

- Wilson, A., (2014) "Loving-Kindness Meditation and Change," Huffington Post, retrieved 12/15/2017, https://www.huffingtonpost.com/kripalu/loving-kindness-meditation_b_3961300.html

- Witvliet, C.V.O., Mohr, A. J. H., Hinman, N. G., & Knoll, R. W. (2015). Transforming or restraining rumination: The impact of compassionate reappraisal versus emotion suppression on empathy, forgiveness, and affective psychophysiology. The Journal of Positive Psychology, 10(3), 248–261. https://doi.org/10.1080/17439760.2014.941381 retrieved 5/27/2020

- Worthington, E. L. Jr., Witvliet, C. V. O., Lerner, A. J., and Scherer, M. (2005). Forgiveness in health research and medical practice. EXPLORE1, 169–176.doi: 10.1016/j.explore.2005.02.012 [accessed Jun 28 2020].

- Worthington, E. L.(2006)Forgiveness and Reconciliation: Theory and Application, Routledge of Taylor & Francis Group, New York

- Worthington, E.L. Jr. & Scherer, M. (2004): Forgiveness is an emotion-focused coping strategy that can reduce health risks and promote health resilience: theory, review, and hypotheses, Psychology & Health, 19:3, 385-405 http://dx.doi.org/10.1080/0887044042000196674 retrieved 8/19/2020

- Worthington, E.L. (2013) Moving Forward: Six Steps to Forgiving Yourself and Breaking Free from the Past http://www.evworthington-forgiveness.com/diy-workbooks retrieved 8/1/2020

- Young, M. A. (2004). *The Community Crisis Response Team Training Manual-Second edition,* National Organization for Victim Assistance, and The Office for Victims of Crime - U.S. Department of Justice, Washington, DC. Retrieved 3/5/03 from www.ojp.usdoj.gov/ovc/publications/infores/crt/

- Your Dictionary (2020) Metaphor Examples, https://examples.yourdictionary.com/metaphor-examples.html retrieved 10/22/2020

PERMISSIONS

I GRATEFULLY ACKNOWLEDGE permission to quote from the following copyrighted works:

- To Paulo Coelho for permission to quote from *By The River Piedra I Sat Down and Wept: A Novel Of Forgiveness*

- To PuddleDancer Press for permission to quote from *Nonviolent Communication- A Language of Compassion* by Dr. Marshall Rosenberg.

- To Rashmi Shetgiri, MD, for the permission to quote and paraphrase her work on Bullying liberally.

- To Dr. Fredric Luskin for permission to quote from *Forgive For Good : A Proven Prescription for Health and Happiness*

INDEX

Notes

Notes

Notes

Printed in Great Britain
by Amazon

70887491R00120